GLORIOUS TRUTHS ABOUT

Mary, Mother of Jesus

GLORIOUS TRUTHS ABOUT
Mary, Mother of Jesus

SUSAN EASTON BLACK

Covenant Communications, Inc.

Cover image: *Mother and Child* © J. Kirk Richards. For information on art prints, visit www.jkirkrichards.com.

Cover design copyright © 2018 by Covenant Communications, Inc.

Published by Covenant Communications, Inc.
American Fork, Utah

Printed in the United States of America
First Printing: November 2018

10 9 8 7 6 5 4 3

ISBN 978-1-52440-870-1

To Arden

My bright and courageous granddaughter

Table of Contents

Introduction

MY PRIMARY PRESIDENT TOOK ASSIGNING parts for the Christmas program seriously and told me more than once, "If you are reverent this year, you will be Mary in the Nativity program." That was the coveted role—the only role for a young girl. Although I tried to be reverent I was never Mary in our ward Christmas program, but one year I *was* cast as a wise man. The program was a success until the Primary president motioned for the wise men to enter the chapel and walk down the aisle to the manger. "It's not time for the wise men to enter," I assured the president. "Jesus was a child when the wise men brought Him gifts. He wasn't lying in a manger." The president must not have heard me, for she motioned for me to walk forward. That year there were only two wise men carrying gifts to Baby Jesus.

I would like to tell my readers that I now choose my battles more wisely, but what I can tell you is that Mary would not have emulated my actions that day in the Christmas program. She was humble, obedient, and willing to do the Lord's will at every turn. She did not question authority, but said instead, "Be it unto me" (Luke 1:38). She was prophetic when she said, "All generations shall call me blessed" (Luke 1:48). The hours of studying her life in preparation for writing this book has inspired me to be better and led me to my knees in prayer as I have realized how much the Savior suffered for me.

It has been a rare privilege to write of Mary, for she was the prophesied virgin chosen to bear the Only Begotten Son of our Eternal Father. She was seen in vision hundreds of years before her birth (see 1 Nephi 11:15). She was the only woman mentioned in holy writ by name before her birth. And she is the only mother who has known the joy of rearing a sinless son.

For these reasons alone, writing a book on the life of Mary has been pure joy. My ability to write of this blessed woman has been greatly enhanced by the talents of my research assistant Eliza Anne Allen, called to be a missionary for The Church of Jesus Christ of Latter-day Saints in Lyon, France. Her mission president doesn't know yet but will soon discover what an absolute jewel has been sent by the Lord to serve with him. To Eliza and to D. Kelly Ogden, my favorite Hebrew scholar, thank you. And to my readers, Mary was not just another virtuous woman who bears a son and passes across the stage of life into anonymity. She was chosen of the Lord before her birth. Her role in the plan of salvation was understood and spoken of by holy prophets. Hers was a life of humble obedience. May my readers find within these pages glorious truths about Mary, the mother of Jesus.

Chapter One

A SINGULAR LIFE

MILLIONS, IF NOT BILLIONS, OF the sons and daughters of God pray to Mary and look to her to better their lives. As Latter-day Saints, we are not numbered among these worshipers. We do not pray to Mary or look to her for miracles and blessings. Christ is at the center of our worship and our lives. We pray to our Father in Heaven in the name of Jesus Christ, not Mary. We seek for the Lord's blessings and long for miracles in our lives in the name of Jesus Christ, not Mary. The question might be asked, what do Latter-day Saints, who profess to be Christians, think of Mary?

First and foremost, all over the world Latter-day Saints acknowledge Mary of Nazareth as the prophesied virgin chosen to bear the Only Begotten Son of our Eternal Father. She was the "virgin, most beautiful and fair" that Nephi saw in vision (1 Nephi 11:15). She was the mother of the "The mighty God, The everlasting Father, The Prince of Peace" prophesied by Isaiah (Isaiah 9:6).

> From Mary, his mother, a mortal woman, [Jesus] inherited the power of mortality, so that he was subject to all the temptations and ills of the flesh, including death itself. From God, his Father, an Immortal Man, he inherited the power of immortality, so that he had power to live forever, or having voluntarily laid down his life, to take it up again in immortal glory.[1]

---

[1] Bruce R. McConkie, "Come, Know the Lord Jesus," General Conference, April 1977.

Second, Mary is the only woman in holy writ mentioned by name before her birth. In 124 BC, as King Benjamin spoke of the Savior's birth, he said, "And his mother shall be called Mary" (Mosiah 3:8). About forty years later, Alma repeated the same message, "And behold, he shall be born of Mary" (Alma 7:10). Thus, Latter-day Saints believe that years before Mary was betrothed to Joseph the carpenter or the angel Gabriel announced she would bear the Son of God, holy men in ancient America were speaking her name.

Third, no other mother on this earth has known the joy of rearing a sinless son—a son whose life was a fulfillment of ancient prophecies that foretold his ministry, atonement, death, and resurrection. Perhaps no other mother has enjoyed the same mother/son bond that she had with Jesus. Elder Bradley D. Foster illustrated that bond by speaking of Mary standing by Jesus at Gethsemane: "In the final, most pivotal moment of His mortal life—after the anguish of Gethsemane, the mock trial, the crown of thorns, the heavy cross to which He was brutally nailed—Jesus looked down from the cross and saw His mother, Mary, who had come to be with her Son."[2]

For these three reasons alone, to Latter-day Saints Mary is not just another virtuous woman. She is the prophesied virgin who gave birth to the Son of God. Because of her singular role as mother of Jesus, Mary stands apart from all other virtuous women who have ever lived.

Although she was subject to temptations, frailties, and the foibles of life like other mortals, Latter-day Saints often look to her as setting a pattern of righteousness worthy of emulation. If looking for an example of humble obedience to the word of God, there are few scriptural accounts better suited than Mary's simple question to the angel Gabriel: "How shall this be, seeing I know not a man?" (Luke 1:34). Mary's question was not one of reticence or doubt, but of sincere curiosity as to how this was to be, for she was a virgin. To Mary's question, the angel answered, "The Holy Ghost shall come upon thee, and the power of the Highest shall overshadow thee: therefore also that holy thing which shall be born of thee shall be called the Son of God" (Luke 1:35). In humble obedience, Mary replied, "Be it unto me according to thy word" (Luke 1:38).

If you need an example of a woman in the scriptures who expressed joy for God's bounteous blessings, consider the vignette of Mary and

[2] Bradley D. Foster, "Mother Told Me," General Conference, April 2010.

Elisabeth. As the expectant mother of John welcomed the expectant mother of the Savior, Mary openly expressed her joy to Elisabeth, exclaiming: "Behold, from henceforth all generations shall call me blessed. For he that is mighty hath done to me great things; and holy is his name" (Luke 1:48–49).

If you're looking for an example of a woman receiving witnesses that her life's choices were in accord with the Lord's will, look no further than Mary. The Gospel writers name Elisabeth and her unborn child, who leaped in her womb, as the first witnesses. Next was Joseph the carpenter, who learned from an angelic messenger in an inspired dream to "fear not to take unto thee Mary thy wife: for that which is conceived in her is of the Holy Ghost. And she shall bring forth a son, and thou shalt call his name JESUS: for he shall save his people from their sins" (Matthew 1:20–21). The third witness were shepherds who found the babe lying in a manger. The fourth and fifth were Simeon and Anna at the temple mount. And the sixth were wise men from the east carrying gifts for the King of Kings. These witnesses, each from various walks and stations in life, must surely have confirmed to Mary her blessed state in the eyes of God.[3]

If there are those who suggest that righteous choices in life and witnesses that attest to those righteous choices should render life's path free of stumbling blocks and strewn with blessings at every turn, look again at the life of Mary. Herod sent soldiers to murder her son. She fled from her homeland to Egypt. She kept the glorious truths about the real parentage of her son from neighbors and perhaps family as Jesus grew from a boy to a man in Nazareth. She became one of His disciples but could not get close to Him due to the pressing crowd. She was at the cross and witnessed her son suffering.

Because of Mary's faithfulness, no matter the personal struggle, it is little wonder that latter-day prophets have suggested that we emulate her life. President Howard W. Hunter said, "Seek to know the will of the Lord in your life, and then say, as did that wonderful exemplar Mary, the mother of Jesus, 'Behold the handmaid of the Lord; be it unto me according to thy word'" (Luke 1:38).[4] President Ezra Taft

---

[3] See Russell M. Nelson, "Woman—Of Infinite Worth," General Conference, October 1989.

[4] Howard W. Hunter, "To the Women of the Church," General Conference, October 1992.

Benson said, "Some Saints are deluded into believing that more and better circumstances will improve their self-image. A positive self-image has little relationship to our material circumstances. Mary, the mother of our Savior, was of most modest circumstances, yet she knew well her responsibility and took joy in it. . . . Her strength was inward, not from outward material things."[5] Relief Society leaders at general conference also suggest applications from Mary's life. Virginia U. Jensen said, "We, like Mary . . . are unique. We have ripples to make and water to share. Given our eternal heritage, we must remember how powerfully our simple, righteous actions can ripple through the hearts and homes of those around us. We have such a great opportunity to do so much good."[6] In quoting Mary's expressions of joy to her cousin Elisabeth, "My soul doth magnify the Lord, "And my spirit hath rejoiced in God, my Savior" (Luke 1:46–47), Naomi M. Shumway pointed out—

> At that moment Mary committed her life to bringing our Savior into mortality, and we as Latter-day Saints know that he had already committed his life unto death for us. When we as women and our girls as daughters of our Heavenly Father fully understand this, then the gospel of Jesus Christ becomes not a religion of habit but one of commitment. . . . We can only be as strong as we must be when we are truly committed.[7]

Because Mary was committed to her role as mother of the Son of God, when latter-day Apostles or prophets list influential women named in the Bible, Mary's name is always included. Elder Jeffrey R. Holland recently said, "To Mother Eve, to Sarah, Rebekah, and Rachel, to Mary of Nazareth . . . I say, 'Thank you for your crucial role in fulfilling the purposes of eternity.'"[8] In President Thomas S. Monson's "private hall of fame reserved exclusively for the real leaders who have influenced the direction of our lives" is Mary, the mother of Jesus. President Monson described her as "the mother of the only sinless man to walk the earth

---

[5] Ezra Taft Benson, "The Honored Place of Woman," General Conference, October 1981.

[6] Virginia U. Jensen, "Ripples," General Conference, October 2000.

[7] Naomi M. Shumway, "Teaching Our Little Women," General Conference, October 1979.

[8] Jeffrey R. Holland, "Behold Thy Mother," General Conference, October 2015.

[and] her acceptance of this sacred and historic role . . . a hallmark of humility."9

I gratefully join with millions of Latter-day Saints to testify that Mary was the prophesied virgin and mother of Jesus Christ. I never cease to marvel at her humble obedience as she submitted her will to the will of God. I am greatly blessed for hours spent studying her life, for it has rekindled affirmation of the singular greatness of her life. I must confess my life is centered on her son, Jesus the Christ. It is Jesus who atoned for my sins. It is Jesus who died and rose the third day as the Resurrected Lord. To this I testify.

---

9 Thomas S. Monson, "My Personal Hall of Fame," General Conference, October 1974.

Chapter Two

ROME RULED JUDAEA WITH AN IRON FIST

"BEHOLD, A VIRGIN SHALL CONCEIVE, and bear a son," prophesied Isaiah (Isaiah 7:14). Nearly two hundred years later in a land less steeped in Israelite tradition, Nephi saw in vision the prophesied virgin "in the city of Nazareth" (1 Nephi 11:13). An angel asked Nephi, "What beholdest thou?" (1 Nephi 11:14). "A virgin, most beautiful and fair above all other virgins," he replied (1 Nephi 11:15). The angel testified to Nephi, "Behold, the virgin whom thou seest is the mother of the Son of God" (1 Nephi 11:18).

Hundreds of years later King Benjamin and Alma spoke her name: "And behold, he [the Son of God] shall be born of Mary" (Mosiah 3:8; Alma 7:10). Yet since the days when holy prophets walked and talked of a Messiah and His mother, years had passed without prophetic fulfillment. Where was that virgin, and more importantly, where was her Son? When Rome ruled Judaea, only a few Israelite maidens still dreamed of being the promised virgin, and even fewer old men dared imagine the birth of a Chosen Son who would be "Wonderful, Counsellor, The mighty God, The everlasting Father, The Prince of Peace" (Isaiah 9:6).

Despair in the holy land of Jerusalem stemmed from centuries of foreign servitude to pagan overlords. As our story begins, it had been nearly a thousand years since one of their own, King David, had ruled over Judaea. Babylon, Egypt, Greece, and Rome had subjected the Judaean population to uncompromising warlords and atrocities inherent in war, bondage, and submission. How could such a downtrodden people still hope for a virgin to conceive and bear a son that had power to release them from oppression?

In Judaea's darkest hour, when Rome ruled over the Holy City with an iron fist and the Roman Emperor Caesar Augustus was acknowledged as a god throughout the empire, the prophecy began to unfold. It is ironic that the background for the prophetic unfolding was in a land dotted with replicas of Caesar's image that were detested by observant Jews as much as what the pagan overlord represented. But there was little fight left in the once-proud people. There had been too many conquerors and too many conquests to rally a formidable insurrection.

Yet thoughts of throwing off the yoke of Caesar Augustus was never far from the lips of the Jews. Along byways and in sequestered homes was heard in whispered tones, "Let my people go"—the same clarion call issued to the Egyptian pharaoh by Moses (see Exodus 7–13). But after centuries of servitude and pleas for heavenly intervention went seemingly unanswered, questions of Jehovah's love for His once-chosen people reared. Could it be that the God of the Judaeans had abandoned or, worse, forgotten His covenant people? The answer was too devastating to really comprehend, for it smacked against the words of holy prophets. However, none could deny that the outward appearance was clear—the light of hope was extinguished when Rome ruled the known world. To rise up and defy the power of the empire was an act of futility that would certainly end in death.

After all, it had been since 63 BC that Syria, which included Judaea at the time, had become a Roman province—one of thirty provinces of an empire that stretched from Britain to the Red Sea and covered about two million square miles. Although there are surely tales of subjection to be told along each mile of rule, the territory that stretched from the slopes of Mount Hermon on the north to the salt pillars bordering the Dead Sea on the south captures our attention, for this land—Judaea—was the home of Mary, the mother of the Son of God. The geographic area was relatively small in comparison to the square miles ruled by Rome, but the area of Judaea—conquered by the Roman General Pompey the Great only three decades before—was one of the most strategic locales in the Roman world.

Due to its key location, the choice of a local leader was all important to the empire. Of all the capable men that could have ruled over Judaea, it is surprising that the Roman choice was Herod, a man of questionable moral character and despised by ardent Jews. But to Caesar Augustus, Herod was an ally of Rome, "an able general, shrewd politician, [and] excellent administrator."[10] Although faithful Christians and Jews today cringe at the mere mention of his name, Herod's hospitality to Roman politicians and soldiers was so lavish and his building efforts so elaborate and extensive that Caesar Augustus was pleased with his choice despite Herod's vicious shortcomings. Caesar quipped of his Roman appointee, "It is better to be Herod's pig than his son."[11] The emperor's quip was an acknowledgment of Herod having executed his sons, and Caesar's wit that as a professed Jew, Herod would never kill and eat a pig.

Herod's reign over Judaea was oppressive to those who longed for a Messiah to deliver them from foreign rule. Nowhere in Judaea were complaints against the Roman appointee louder than in Jerusalem, a city named for peace and built on the sacred site of ancient Salem—the City of Holiness. Complaints centered on what inhabitants perceived as Herod's purposeful defilement of the Holy City, his ordering of Roman soldiers into the city, and his blatant decision to destroy the genealogical registers of the temple. Such egregious actions angered worshipers of Jehovah to such an extent that dislike, distrust, and even hatred of Herod reached an unchecked feverish pitch in the Holy City.[12]

It was in those days—days when Herod outwardly professed to be a worshiper of Jehovah but was inwardly a man of despicable moral character—the Gospel writer Luke begins his account of the wondrous, even miraculous events in Jerusalem that led to the birth of the Messiah. Luke opens his account with a dramatic appearance of an angel sent from Jehovah to the elderly priest Zacharias and to "a virgin, most beautiful and fair above all other virgins" (1 Nephi 11:15). This dramatic beginning, against a backdrop of despotism of Herod and the iron rule of

---

[10] National Geographic Society, *Everyday Life in Bible Times* (Washington, DC: National Geographic Society, 1967), 296–297; Peter Connolly, *A History of the Jewish People in the Time of Jesus from Herod the Great to Masada* (New York: Peter Bedrick Books, 1983), 16.

[11] Bruce R. McConkie, *Mortal Messiah: From Bethlehem to Calvary.* 4 vols. (Salt Lake City: Deseret Book, 1981), 1:362; Wolfgang Pax, *Footsteps of Jesus* (Jerusalem: Nateev Publishing, 1970), 28.

[12] Kaari Ward, ed., *Jesus and His Times* (Pleasantville, New York: Reader's Digest, 1990), 14, 40–42, 203; McConkie, *Mortal Messiah*, 1:86; David B. Galbraith, D. Kelly Ogden, and Andrew C. Skinner, *Jerusalem, The Eternal City* (Salt Lake City: Deseret Book, 1996), 153–154.

Rome, is a compelling story, for against great odds in a land riddled with strife and servitude the ancient prophecy of Isaiah was beginning to be fulfilled.

We know not how it was done any more than we comprehend the Creation or how the heavens began. Yet we know that a Child born of a virgin named Mary on the outskirts of Bethlehem was the prophesied "Wonderful, Counsellor, The mighty God, The everlasting Father, The Prince of Peace" (Isaiah 9:6). Although the Child would be "despised and rejected of men" and would grow to be "a man of sorrows, and acquainted with grief," He was the prophesied Child born of a virgin who would triumph over all enemies, conquer death, and rise the third day as the Resurrected Lord (Isaiah 53:3).

With the mere stroke of a pen, the physician Luke turns the attention of the world from the mighty Caesar Augustus and the cruel Herod to an elderly priest named Zacharias, whose name means "Jehovah has remembered."[13] Zacharias belonged to the priestly course/quorum of Abia (Abijah). Priests in his course resided near Jerusalem in the hill country of Judaea and journeyed to the Holy City to officiate in priestly duties on the Temple Mount. They officiated each year in the temple for six days and two Sabbaths during the Jewish months that correspond to our April and October.

The course of Abia began their priestly duties on the Temple Mount by assembling in the Hall of Polished Stones to offer prescribed prayers to Jehovah: "With great love hast Thou loved us, O Lord our God, and with much overflowing pity has Thou pitied us . . . Blessed be the Lord, who in love chose His people Israel."[14] After prayers, the assembled priests repeated the *Shema*, the Hebrew creed or belief that begins, "Hear, O Israel: The Lord our God is one Lord" (see Deuteronomy 6:4-9;

---

[13] McConkie, *Mortal Messiah*, 1:304–305; Alfred Edersheim, *The Temple: In Ministry and Services as They Were at the Time of Christ* (Grand Rapids, Michigan: Wm. B. Eerdmans Publishing Company, 1994), 87; Alfred Edersheim, *Sketches of Jewish Social Life* (Peabody, Massachusetts: Hendrickson Publishers, Inc., 1994), 37; J. R. Dummelow, *A Commentary on the Holy Bible* (New York City: Macmillan, 1964), 737.

[14] E. J. Tinsley, "The Gospel According to Luke." In R. Ackroyd, A. R. C. Leaney, J. W. Packer, eds., *The Cambridge Bible Commentary* (New York: Cambridge University Press, 1965), 165–166.

11:13–21; Numbers 15:37–41). This was followed by the casting of lots to determine which priest would have the singular privilege of burning incense on the golden altar in the Holy Temple each day of the week the course of Abia served on the Temple Mount.

According to the Gospel of Luke, not by chance but by divine plan the lot on this sacred week fell upon Zacharias (see Luke 1:9). Although elderly, he was not disqualified by age or infirmity from the honor. According to Jewish tradition, Zacharias chose two assistants to prepare the sacred rite of incense. The assistants went inside the Holy Temple, where they removed debris from the altar before spreading live coals on the altar. When the assistants' duties were completed, they worshiped before the altar and then retired from the temple. Their exit from the sanctuary alerted Zacharias that all was in readiness for him to enter.[15]

Tradition suggests that Zacharias walked up the temple steps alone and entered the temple to spread incense over the hot coals on the altar (see Psalms 141:2). After entering the temple, Zacharias parted an embroidered veil that concealed the altar of incense, a seven-branched candelabrum, and a table on which lay twelve loaves of shewbread, each loaf representing a tribe in the house of Israel. Behind another curtain that Zacharias was not allowed to enter lay the Holy of Holies. Only on the Day of Atonement could a high priest—not a priest from the course of Abia—enter the Holy of Holies, which symbolically meant entering the presence of God.

Zacharias would have stood alone between the curtains, facing the altar to his west. To his north was the table of shewbread, and to his south stood a golden candelabrum. There he would wait until a signal from a ram horn was blown, marking "the time of incense had come."[16] The signal would also alert priests serving in the Holy Temple to leave the inner court and prostrate themselves on the temple grounds in silent worship. After hearing the signal, it is presumed that Zacharias would have spread incense on the altar. It was customary that when the priest saw incense kindling on the hot coals, he bowed down in worship and withdrew from the holy area. Such was not the case that day with Zacharias.

---

15 Tinsley, "The Gospel According to Luke," 165–166.

16 Pax, *Footsteps of Jesus*, 70–71; Alfred Edersheim, *Jesus the Messiah: An Abridged Edition of the Life and Times of Jesus the Messiah* (Grand Rapids: Wm. B. Eerdmans Publishing, 1976), 3–4; Edersheim, *Temple*, 167.

Seeing a heavenly messenger sent from the presence of God "standing on the right side of the altar of incense" arrested Zacharias's steps (Luke 1:11). The angel was Gabriel, known in mortality as Noah. Of the authority resting upon Gabriel, the Prophet Joseph Smith said, "The priesthood was first given to Adam. . . . Then to Noah, who is Gabriel; he stands next in authority to Adam in the Priesthood. . . . These men held keys first on earth, and then in heaven."[17] It is not surprising that "when Zacharias saw [the angel], he was troubled, and fear fell upon him," for never had an angel been seen in the holy temple (Luke 1:12).

"Fear not, Zacharias," said angel Gabriel to the trembling priest (Luke 1:13):

Thy prayer is heard; and thy wife Elisabeth shall bear thee a son, and thou shalt call his name John.

And thou shalt have joy and gladness; and many shall rejoice at his birth.

For he shall be great in the sight of the Lord . . . and he shall be filled with the Holy Ghost, even from his mother's womb.

And many of the children of Israel shall he turn to the Lord their God. (Luke 1:13–16.)

The angel then declared that the prophesied child would go before the Messiah to prepare a people for the coming of the Lord (see Luke 1:17).

"Whereby shall I know this?" asked Zacharias of the angel Gabriel, explaining, "I am an old man, and my wife well stricken in years" (Luke 1:18). The angel answered,

I am Gabriel, that stand in the presence of God; and am sent to speak unto thee, and to shew thee these glad tidings.

And, behold, thou shalt be dumb, and not able to speak, until the day that these things shall be performed, because thou believest not my words, which shall be fulfilled in their season. (Luke 1:19–20.)

---

[17] Joseph Smith Discourse, between circa 26 June and circa 4 August 1839-A. As Reported by Willard Richards, Joseph Smith Papers, 63.

As Zacharias conversed with the angel and seemingly delayed his exit from the temple, his fellow priests, who had prostrated themselves on the ground in worship, "marvelled that he tarried so long" (Luke 1:21). When Zacharias finally emerged from the holy edifice and was unable to speak, the priests "perceived that he had seen a vision in the temple: for he beckoned unto them, and [yet] remained speechless" (Luke 1:22). Zacharias was unable to tell his brethren that a forerunner would be conceived—a child of promise was to be born. He was unable to speak of an Elias coming to prepare a suffering people for the prophesied Savior of the World—the Messiah—or of his role and that of Elisabeth.

And thus our story begins. It begins with an angel that had more than one errand to fulfill. The angel Gabriel, who had announced the birth of an Elias to Zacharias, must now go to the small village of Nazareth to speak to "a virgin, most beautiful and fair above all other virgins" (1 Nephi 11:15). Had Mary dreamed of being the promised virgin who "shall conceive, and bear a son" (Isaiah 7:14)? It is presumed that she, like other maidens in Israel, dared not imagine the ancient prophecy could be fulfilled when Roman overlords ruled Judaea.

Chapter Three

A VIRGIN MOST FAIR

THE GOSPEL WRITER LUKE ABRUPTLY leaves the account of Zacharias, Elisabeth, and their unborn child to proclaim the time has arrived when an angel will announce "a virgin shall conceive" and become the mother of the prophesied Son of God (Isaiah 7:14). Luke's recounting of the angelic declaration to Mary is not a declaration to an aging woman like Elisabeth, Sarah, or the barren Hannah, "whose pleas for a child will finally be answered." In fact, "Mary does not fit the pattern of the elderly barren women of the Old Testament, and she makes no request of God for the gift of a child."[18] Luke's account of the chosen maiden is set in a backdrop of fearful yesteryears when Augustus Caesar and his Roman appointee Herod ruled with unrelenting tyranny. Luke features a limestone cave, an unlikely crib, lowly shepherds, and wise men who follow a star. For those who have not read the story, it is a page-turner even for unbelievers.

Luke begins his wondrous account by declaring, "In the sixth month the angel Gabriel was sent from God unto a city of Galilee, named Nazareth" located on the foothills of lower Galilee, the ancient land of the tribe of Zebulon (Luke 1:26). The name *Nazareth* is derived from a Hebrew word meaning "guard place" or "watch tower," suggesting that the village was once an outpost of a nearby town.[19] Anciently, the village

---

[18] Beverly Roberts Gaventa, *Mary, Glimpses of the Mother of Jesus* (Columbia, South Carolina: University of South Carolina Press, 1995), 52.

[19] Ward, *Jesus and His Times*, 92, 311; LaMar C. Berrett and D. Kelly Ogden, *Discovering the World of the Bible* (Provo, Utah: Grandin Book, 1996), 110; R. Ackroyd, A. R. C. Leaney, and J. W. Packer, ed., *According to Matthew* (London: Cambridge University Press, 1963), 34.

of Nazareth was so unimportant that it is not mentioned in the Old
Testament, the *Talmud*, or by the Jewish historian Josephus. Yet to the
Gospel writer Luke, Nazareth is all important, for it was the village of the
young maiden Mary.

At the time of the angelic appearance to Mary, Nazareth boasted of
fewer than four hundred people residing in approximately seventy-five
residential homes. The village was small, indeed, when compared to the
holy city of Jerusalem and the capital of the Roman Empire—Rome.
An angelic appearance in a village of such little consequence is in stark
contrast to the Temple Mount on which Gabriel spoke to the priest
Zacharias. Likewise, a young woman, whose adventures in life were
few, contrasts greatly with the elderly priest who had spent a lifetime
performing priestly duties on the Temple Mount and in worship of
Jehovah. Yet it was to the young maiden Mary, "destined to be the
mother of the only sinless man to walk the earth," that the angel Gabriel
appeared.[20] Thus, in the sequestered village of Nazareth that was just a
spot on a map then as now, a young woman with a common name, Mary,
had a heavenly experience that changed her life and the destiny of the
world forever.

As Mary enters the scene, Luke fails to write of her parents or
siblings. He informs his readers that she is espoused to Joseph the
carpenter, which makes Joseph the only familial name associated with
Mary.[21] The phrase "the carpenter" attached to his name is significant, for
it signifies that Joseph chose to be a tradesman rather than a government
official. If Judaea had been independent of foreign rule, a tradesman
might have carried with it an inferior social status or denoted a man with
a "voluntary or necessary preoccupation with the things of this world that
perish with the using."[22] Since Judaea—or what Rome called Palestine—
had been ruled by foreigners for centuries, being a tradesman was extolled
in small Jewish villages like Nazareth, for it was one way an ardent Jew
could show his manly independence.

---

[20] Thomas S. Monson, "My Personal Hall of Fame," General Conference, October
1974.

[21] Gaventa, *Mary, Glimpses of the Mother of Jesus*, 52.

[22] Edersheim, *Sketches of Jewish Life*, 182; Ward, *Jesus and His Times*, 76–77, 91,
202.

Most trades in Nazareth, like carpentry, were family enterprises that had passed from father to son for generations. Members of competing or similar trades did business in the same geographic areas of Jewish society, much like their fathers before them. For example, in Jerusalem there was a street occupied by butchers, one by bakers, and another by ironsmiths. The craftsmen in Jerusalem as well as Nazareth wore a sign of their trade while walking through the marketplace. It was not unusual to see a dyer wearing a brightly colored cloth, a tailor with a large bone needle in his cloak, or a public writer with a wooden ruler behind his ear.[23] And as a carpenter, Joseph wore a wood chip behind his ear.

Since Luke wants his readers to know that Mary was espoused to Joseph the carpenter, it can only be assumed that she and Joseph followed marriage customs dictated by the Mosaic Law. The law regarded a betrothal (also known as an *espousal* or an *erusin*) as a solemn agreement, a covenant between a man and a woman.[24] The typical Jewish man was age twenty at the time of his betrothal. Jewish women were betrothed at a younger age, as young as twelve years old. We assume that Joseph and Mary were near these ages even though apocryphal accounts depict Joseph as an elderly widower.[25]

If, indeed, Mary and Joseph followed Jewish protocol in their betrothal, it was not infrequent that the ceremony took place in the home of the betrothed-to-be. In that house, a tent or booth was raised before the formal betrothal ceremony began. Inside the makeshift structure, the making sacred or promising of the woman to the man occurred in front of witnesses, who gathered to mark the occasion and later attested that the young woman was promised to the man. Witnesses watched as the man gave the young woman a piece of money or its equivalency

---

[23] Edersheim, *Sketches of Jewish Life*, 182; Ward, *Jesus and His Times*, 76–77, 91, 202.

[24] "The Story of Mary: From the Biblical World to Today," *National Geographic* (Washington, DC: Time Inc., 2018), 14.

[25] James E. Talmage, *Jesus the Christ* (Salt Lake City: Deseret Book, 1981), 84; McConkie, *Mortal Messiah*, 1:223; Ralph Gower, *The New Manners and Customs of Bible Times* (Chicago: Moody Press, 1987), 65.

and said, "Lo, thou art betrothed unto me."[26] A written document that bore his words and the woman's name provided additional proof of the ceremony. The betrothal ceremony ended with a benediction: "Blessed art Thou, O Lord our God, King of the World, Who hath sanctified us by His Commandments."[27] When the formalities ended, it is assumed the witnesses and later villagers rejoiced with the young maiden—in this case Mary, for she was promised to Joseph the carpenter—and within a year wedding festivities would celebrate their union.

During that year, Mary was known as the wife of Joseph and wore a veil when venturing out-of-doors. Joseph was known as her husband. Even though Mary was his wife, she would continue to live with her family or friends and all communication between herself and Joseph would have been through significant others. If Joseph had died during the espousal period, Mary would have been known as his widow. If Mary had died, Joseph would have been known as a widower. Any unfaithfulness during the period by either Joseph or Mary would have been denounced as adultery by the Jewish society. According to Deuteronomy 22:23–24, the penalty for adultery was death.

As Joseph prepared a home for Mary and she prepared her wedding clothes, perhaps Mary imagined her destiny only in terms of her betrothal, her upcoming wedding, and festivities surrounding the day she would be a bride. If she had such thoughts, they soon changed, for the angel Gabriel was "sent from God" to bring her glad tidings of great joy (Luke 1:26).

"Hail, thou that art high favoured, the Lord is with thee: blessed art thou among women," Gabriel announced to Mary (Luke 1:28). According to the Latin Vulgate version of the Bible, "hail" is translated as *Ave*, which forms the phrase, "Ave Maria." The phrase *highly favoured* means "imbued or endowed with grace from God" (Luke 1:28).[28]

The greeting, although glorious, was troubling to Mary. Her reaction to such high praise is recorded in the Gospel of Luke as "fear" (Luke 1:30).

---

[26] Talmage, *Jesus the Christ*, 84; McConkie, *Mortal Messiah*, 1:223; Gower, *New Manners and Customs*, 65.

[27] Bruce E. Dana, *Mary, Mother of Jesus* (Springville, Utah: Cedar Fort Books, Inc., 2001), 36.

[28] Talmage, *Jesus the Christ*, 77; Pax, *Footsteps of Jesus*, 22.

Another way to translate her reaction is "awe," revealing Mary's innate humility and limited understanding of why she was chosen to be the prophesied virgin (see Luke 1:28–30).

"Fear not, Mary: for thou hast found favour with God," the angel proclaimed (Luke 1:30). Note that Gabriel does not explain to Mary why she has "found favor with God." This contrasts with Zacharias and Elisabeth, who were "both righteous before God, walking in all the commandments and ordinances of the Lord blameless" (Luke 1:6). It is easy to conclude that Zacharias and Elisabeth had found favor with God because of their actions. In the case of Mary, there is no explanation as to how she arrived at her favorable standing.

Gabriel announces: "And, behold, thou shalt conceive in thy womb, and bring forth a son" (Luke 1:31).[29] The son was to be begotten of the Eternal Father. According to Elder James E. Talmage, "Not in violation of natural law but in accordance with a higher manifestation thereof; and, the offspring from that association of supreme sanctity, celestial Sireship, and pure though mortal maternity was of right to be called the 'Son of the Highest.'"[30] This most sacred event is berated by unbelieving scholars as an imitation of Greek and Roman mythology that depicts gods "consorting with mortal women" and siring children.[31] The sacred angelic pronouncement was not an imitation of mythology, but the basis for the belief that Jesus is the Son of God.

The angel also told Mary that she was to "call his name JESUS. He shall be great, and shall be called the Son of the Highest: and the Lord God shall give unto him the throne of his father David: And he shall reign over the house of Jacob for ever; and of his kingdom there shall be no end" (Luke 1:31–33). The name *Jesus* is the Hebrew equivalent of *Yehoshua* and *Jeshua*, meaning "Jehovah is salvation." The Hebrew/

---

[29] Gaventa, *Mary, Glimpses of the Mother*, 53.

[30] Talmage, *Jesus the Christ*, 77; see William Smith, *The New Smith's Bible Dictionary*, Reuel G. Lemmons, ed. (Garden City, New York: Doubleday & Company, 1966), 238; *The Life and Teachings of Jesus and His Apostles*, prepared by the Church Education System, 2d ed., rev. (Salt Lake City: The Church of Jesus Christ of Latter-day Saints, 1979), 23; Louis Jacobs, *The Book of Jewish Beliefs* (West Orange, New Jersey: Behrman House, 1984), 174; Pax, *In the Footsteps of Jesus*, 22.

[31] Smith, *Bible Dictionary*, 238; *Life and Teachings of Jesus*, 23; Talmage, *Jesus the Christ*, 77; Jacobs, *Book of Jewish Beliefs*, 174; Pax, *Footsteps of Jesus*, 22.

Aramaic term for *Messiah* is "anointed one," whereas the corresponding word in Greek is "Christ." The phrase *Jesus the Christ* comes from combining the Hebrew name with the Greek title.[32]

Being concerned over her ability to bear a son, Mary asked the angel, "How shall this be, seeing I know not a man?" (Luke 1:34). Her question simply put was, "How can a virgin conceive?" The angel's explanation was to speak of the omnipotent power of God: "The Holy Ghost shall come upon thee, and the power of the Highest shall overshadow thee" (Luke 1:35). As Mary thought about the explanation, Gabriel assured her that "with God nothing shall be impossible" (Luke 1:37). By way of example, Gabriel then told Mary of a kinswoman beyond her childbearing years: "Thy cousin Elisabeth, she hath also conceived a son in her old age: and this is the sixth month with her, who was called barren" (Luke 1:36).

The kinship bond between Mary and Elisabeth remains obscured. In the King James Version of the Bible, Elisabeth is referred to as "thy kinswoman" and "thy cousin." It was John Wycliffe, the father of the English Bible, who suggested a cousin relationship between the two women.[33] The Greek translation suggests only a familial relationship.

Being endowed with grace from God, Mary replied to Gabriel, "Behold the handmaid of the Lord; be it unto me according to thy word" (Luke 1:38). Mary's reply to the angelic pronouncement reveals her humility and her willingness to be the handmaiden of the Lord, the prophesied virgin to bear the Son of God, or as President Thomas S. Monson said, "Her acceptance of this sacred and historic role is a hallmark of humility."[34] We hesitate to intrude upon the sacred circumstances surrounding the conception except to say the child conceived in Mary's womb was the Son of God—a Son that would be "a light to lighten the Gentiles, and the glory of [Jehovah's] people Israel" (Luke 2:32).

For this chosen mother, the years following the Savior's birth would not be easy. They would be fraught with an escape to Egypt, losing Him

---

[32] Smith, *Bible Dictionary*, 238; *Life and Teachings of Jesus*, 23; Talmage, *Jesus the Christ*, 77; Jacobs, *Book of Jewish Beliefs*, 174; Pax, *Footsteps of Jesus*, 22.

[33] Pax, *Footsteps of Jesus*, 22; Alfred Edersheim, *The Life and Times of Jesus the Messiah* (Peabody, Massachusetts: Hendrickson Publishers, Inc., 1995), 110; Dummelow, *Bible Commentary*, 739.

[34] Monson, "My Personal Hall of Fame," General Conference, October 1974.

on the Temple Mount, and watching Him endure mockery, thorns, and a cross. But on this night, when the angel spoke of Mary as the chosen vessel of the Lord to bear the Son of God, she was not troubled by thoughts of harm to her child. She was confident in the Lord's love. In the words of President Russell M. Nelson, "[She was] the perfect example of complete submission to the will of God."[35]

When the angelic visitation ended, Mary arose and went in haste "into a city of Juda" to find Elisabeth, a kinswoman who also carried a child of promise in her womb (Luke 1:39). Artists and storytellers would have us believe that Mary traveled alone to the hill country of Juda, nearly a hundred miles from Nazareth. Such was not the case. It was dangerous for a Jewish woman—especially a beautiful veiled woman—to journey alone from one community to another when Rome occupied Judaea. If Mary had journeyed alone, she might have fallen prey to soldiers, transients, or robbers on the road between Nazareth and Juda. Although the road was a popular highway for pilgrims and caravans, there were dangers for those who traveled alone.[36] Wise travelers, especially women, chose narrow paths. "The road is safe. Everything will be all right. Even your feet will not strike a stone" was an ancient eastern farewell expressed to those who ventured on narrow paths.[37]

The narrow path, unknown to robbers and murderers, was not easy. The route usually took longer than traveling on broad paths and led travelers over steep climbs and rocky terrain. Symbolically, the narrow path leads to heaven while the wide highway leads to destruction. The passage in Matthew, "Narrow is the way, which leadeth unto life, and few there be that find it," in Aramaic reads, "Oh how narrow is the road and how few are found on it" (Matthew 7:14). It is likely that Mary was accompanied by family or friends as she journeyed on a narrow path to the home of Zacharias and Elisabeth.

Although tradition suggests that Mary and her entourage stopped at a spring located west of Jerusalem in Ein Kerem for a cool drink, the Gospel writer Luke tells only of Mary going to the "house of Zacharias,

---

[35] Nelson, "Woman—Of Infinite Worth," General Conference, October 1989.

[36] Pax, *Footsteps of Jesus*, 22; Edersheim, *Times of Jesus*, 110; Dummelow, *Bible Commentary*, 739.

[37] George M. Lamsa, *Gospel Light: Comments on the Teachings of Jesus from Aramaic and Unchanged Eastern Customs* (Philadelphia: A. J. Holman Company, Bible Publishers, 1936), 55, 231.

and saluted Elisabeth" (Luke 1:40).[38] Why not salute Zacharias? The angelic message, "Fear not, Zacharias: for thy prayer is heard; and thy wife Elisabeth shall bear thee a son," had left him in speechless silence (Luke 1:13).

Elisabeth knew, without conversing with Mary, of her blessed state. "Blessed art thou among women, and blessed is the fruit of thy womb," Elisabeth exclaimed (Luke 1:42). The child Elisabeth carried in her womb also acknowledged the mother of the Son of God. The unborn child leaped, and as he did Elisabeth was "filled with the Holy Ghost" (Luke 1:41). The account of the expectant mother of John extending a greeting to the expectant mother of the Messiah is a singular event in holy writ, or as Elder Neal A. Maxwell asked, "What greater conversation of anticipation has there been than that of Elisabeth and Mary when also the babe in Elisabeth leaped in recognition of Mary?"[39] It was "the salutation of the young mother to the aged mother, when two women, alone in the hill-country, carried the destinies of the world."[40]

Of significant importance is the fact that in both annunciation accounts—Zacharias and Mary—the announcements addressed the future greatness of John and Jesus.[41] As Elisabeth speaks to Mary, the text is written as if the birth had already occurred, for Mary is addressed as "Mother"—as if the future is present. Elisabeth wondered aloud, "[Why] the mother of my Lord should come to me?" (Luke 1:43). Elizabeth's wonderment praises Mary, but notice in Mary's response she praises God: "My soul doth magnify the Lord, And my spirit hath rejoiced in God my Saviour . . . from henceforth all generations shall call me blessed. For he that is mighty hath done to me great things; and holy is his name" (Luke 1:46–49).

As Mary speaks to Elisabeth, her words echo the sayings of prophets and the Song of Hannah (see 1 Samuel 2:1–10). In Mary's words, she adds insight into the marvelous power of God in ages past. In so doing, Mary becomes an interpreter of the Gospel: "[The Lord] hath scattered the proud in the imagination of their hearts. He hath put down the

---

[38] "The Story of Mary," *National Geographic*, 35.

[39] Elder Neal A. Maxwell, "The Women of God," General Conference, April 1978.

[40] Alice Meynell, *Mary, the Mother of Jesus* (London and Boston: The Medici Society, 1925), 9.

[41] Gaventa, *Mary, Glimpses of the Mother*, 58.

mighty from their seats, and exalted them of low degree. He hath filled the hungry with good things; and the rich he hath sent empty away" (Luke 1:51–53).[42] After citing the wonders and greatness of Jehovah, Mary ends her reflection of God's power by humbly acknowledging that the most miraculous of all His powerful actions is that the Great Jehovah has been mindful of her. In these words, Mary reveals her exquisite joy in being chosen to bear the Son of God.

In her rejoicing there is no hint of reservation, selfish concern, fear, or pride—only confidence that "with God nothing shall be impossible" (Luke 1:37). Unfortunately, her joyous expressions fade quickly as she returns to Nazareth.

---

[42] Gaventa, *Mary, Glimpses of the Mother*, 58.

Chapter Four

THE ROAD TO BETHLEHEM

===

AFTER A PROLONGED ABSENCE OF three months, Mary returned to her village of Nazareth. Not surprising, her return was unsettling to Joseph. Mary was with child, a forbidden breach of their betrothal vow. According to Deuteronomy 24:1, legal action was needed to end the betrothal, and Mary's pregnancy was sufficient legal grounds for divorce. When Jewish law prevailed, if a betrothed wife was discovered to be unfaithful to her husband, she was put to death unless she had been forcibly raped (see Deuteronomy 22:23–27). The presumed licentious behavior that led to Mary's pregnancy demanded an immediate end of the betrothal and the requisite punishment prescribed by Jewish law.

The decision facing Joseph was not if he should end the betrothal, but how. Would he choose to end his union with Mary by public notice—a trial before three judges in the local synagogue, where testimonies were openly expressed and a judgment rendered? If Mary were found guilty of adultery, she would not be put to death as demanded by Jewish law because Rome would not allow such punishment for fornication or adultery. However, public humiliation in the small community of Nazareth would follow Mary all her days. The other choice facing Joseph was a private agreement—a written document known as a bill of divorce or certificate of dismissal signed by witnesses (see Matthew 1:19). The witnesses could be Joseph's choice, such as close family members, and the reason for divorce kept from civil authorities and public notice (see

Deuteronomy 24:1). The divorce could then be a family secret never openly discussed.[43]

As Joseph weighed the matter, he was of a mind to "put [Mary] away privily," as the Gospel writer Matthew penned, "Joseph her husband, being a just man, and not willing to make her a publick example, was minded to put her away privily" (Matthew 1:19). Although Joseph was about to make the merciful choice in this instance, such was not the mind or will of God.

It is not known how long Joseph pondered over ending his betrothal to Mary before he had an inspired dream. An angel of the Lord appeared to him in the dream and said, "Joseph, thou son of David, fear not to take unto thee Mary thy wife: for that which is conceived in her is of the Holy Ghost. And [Mary] shall bring forth a son, and thou shalt call his name JESUS: for he shall save his people from their sins" (Matthew 1:20–21). The dream was not only informative to Joseph regarding Mary's pregnancy, but according to Jewish tradition, it was a sign of God's favor to him. With the angelic appearance and directive to Joseph, it would have been unwise for him to unduly postpone obedience to the command. It was a known fact among Israelite males that to thwart or put off the Lord's favor—instructions presented in a good dream—was to reap the whirlwind of His wrath.[44]

Joseph's relief in knowing the parentage of the unborn child is not recorded in the Gospels. We can only assume that any misgivings he may have nurtured gave way to unspeakable joy as he learned that his beloved Mary was to be the prophesied mother of the Son of God, the Hope of Israel, the Messiah who would rid Judaea of foreign rule. Joseph surely realized from the dream that he, a mere carpenter, would become the provider and protector of both mother and child. His was a unique opportunity—a daunting responsibility that would challenge the best of any Israelite male. Joseph was to share with Mary in the sacred privilege of rearing the Only Begotten Son of God.

Although his thoughts are not recorded, Joseph, like Mary had three months earlier, arose and "did as the angel of the Lord had bidden him, and

---

[43] Ward, *Jesus and His Times*, 16, 76; Talmage, *Jesus the Christ*, 79; John J. Rousseau and Rami Arav, *Jesus and His World: An Archaeological and Cultural Dictionary* (Minneapolis: Augsburg Fortress Press, 1995), 275.

[44] Edersheim, *Jesus the Messiah*, 11; Edersheim, *Sketches of Jewish Life*, 139; Pax, *Footsteps of Jesus*, 89.

took unto him his wife" (Matthew 1:24). In so doing, Mary and Joseph must surely have participated in the traditional Jewish wedding festivities. Such festivities would have occurred before Mary accompanied Joseph to Bethlehem, for Jewish custom forbad a betrothed wife from accompanying her husband on any such journey without a formal wedding vow.

Jewish tradition favors Mary and Joseph being wed on the third day of the week (see Genesis 1: 9–13). Basis for the tradition stems from the Creation account in the book of Genesis, in which the word *good* appears twice in the description of God's creations on the third day. Because of repetition, Jews believed that marriages celebrated on the third day of the week received a double blessing from Jehovah.[45]

Whether the third day of the week or another, on that special day in Nazareth, Joseph was the groom and Mary, his bride. Not knowing the particulars of their wedding day, we turn to tales of Jewish wedding festivities.

With myrtle garland atop his head as a symbol of love, the groom left his home to search the village to find his bride. Friends, carrying lighted torches, followed behind him in hopes of being some help in the search. The groom's quest always ended at the bride's parental home. There the groom exclaimed to boisterous friends, "Come see the treasure I have found." The groom then lifted the veil from his bride's face and laid it upon his shoulder. His words and actions led villagers to joyously declare, "The government shall be upon his shoulder," meaning the groom has the right to begin a family in the house of Israel.

As excitement mounted, the groom took the hand of his bride and led her in a festive procession towards her new home. Villagers walking behind played music, danced, and waved flowers and myrtle branches in celebration of the upcoming wedding. When the bride and groom arrived at their new home, villagers shouted, "Take her according to the Law of Moses and of Israel."[46]

Their words signaled it was time for the wedding ceremony—the *nissuin*—to begin. In the ceremony, the festive couple were encircled by

[45] Edersheim, *Jesus the Messiah*, 11; Edersheim, *Sketches of Jewish Life*, 139; Rousseau and Arav, *Jesus and His World*, 39.

[46] Edersheim, *Sketches of Jewish Life*, 140; Ward, *Jesus and His Times*, 115; Edersheim, *Jesus the Messiah*, 69–71; James Harpur, *The Miracles of Jesus* (London: Reader's Digest, 1997), 11; Abraham Joshua Heschel, *The Sabbath: Its Meaning for Modern Man* (New York City: Noonday Press, 1951), 108.

guests under a wedding canopy, crowned with garlands, and pronounced king and queen respectively. After signing the *Kethubah*, stipulating the "bridegroom undertook to work for her, to honour, keep, and care for her, as is the manner of the men of Israel," the marriage feast began—a celebration that often lasted for a week or two.[47]

Although the Gospel writer Luke failed to mention wedding festivities in his narrative of Mary and Joseph, he was not silent concerning the overarching power of Rome or the "decree from Caesar Augustus, that all the world should be taxed" (Luke 2:1). A decree from Caesar was not to be ignored, even by newlyweds. The ruler's royal whims, no matter how repugnant to his Jewish subjects, were not to be denied. After generations of violently enforced subjugation and Roman taxation, Jewish men reluctantly complied with the imperial decree. Many journeyed more than a hundred miles to register in ancient family lands, an important first phase of Caesar's taxation process.[48] In their compliance to Caesar's decree, the prophecies of the greatness of Israel and the coming of a Messiah seemed lost on the world stage of Rome.[49]

Yet among the thousands on the move throughout Judaea was Joseph the carpenter and his wife Mary, "being great with child" (Luke 2:5). They were heading toward Bethlehem of Judaea, first mentioned in Genesis: "And Rachel died, and was buried in the way to Ephrath, which is Bethlehem" (Genesis 35:19). In the fields east of Bethlehem, Ruth met Boaz, and from their union came Jesse, father of King David. In those fields young David tended his sheep and dwelt among his kin.

As for Mary and Joseph, their journey took them nearly ninety miles or five days from Nazareth to the outskirts of Bethlehem—the family land of the house of David built on a terraced countryside about five miles from the holy city of Jerusalem. It is not known which route Mary and Joseph took to reach Bethlehem. They either took a direct route through Samaria or a route through Jericho and the Judaean desert. However, it is known that by journeying to Bethlehem they fulfilled the prophecy of Isaiah, who

---

[47] Dana, *Mary, Mother of Jesus*, 80.

[48] Edersheim, *Jesus the Messiah*, 13; Raymond E. Brown, *Birth of the Messiah—A Commentary on the Infancy Narratives in the Gospels of Matthew and Luke* (New York: Doubleday, 1993), 412–418; Smith, *Bible Dictionary*, 35; Pax, *Footsteps of Jesus*, 28, 34; *Life and Teachings*, 28–29.

[49] Gaventa, *Glimpses of the Mother*, 59.

wrote of the Messiah being born in the homeland of David, Bethlehem of Judaea (see Isaiah 9:1, 6–7; 11:1, 10).[50]

When Mary and Joseph arrived in the prophesied town, they found no room in the inn. The Greek word for inn is *khan*, meaning "guest chamber" or "room for rent in a private house." The word for inn does not mean a caravansary, which was a sun-dried brick, rectangular-shaped building near Bethlehem constructed to accommodate travelers traversing the route between Jerusalem and Egypt. According to tradition, rooms, storage chambers, and stalls in the caravansary surrounded a central courtyard. Inside the courtyard was a well, used by travelers to fill water bags and to water their livestock. If travelers reached the caravansary early in the day, they were welcomed by an innkeeper. If they arrived in the evening, the caravansary door was closed for protection, and travelers were encouraged to move along. The reason for the closure had everything to do with the darkness of night. In darkness, it was difficult to identify whether the traveler was a Gentile or, worse, a Roman soldier.[51]

It is unlikely that Joseph sought shelter for Mary in the public, noisy caravansary. It is more probable that he looked for a private room to rent in Bethlehem but "there was no room for them" (Luke 2:7). Failing to find such a room, Mary and Joseph lodged in a nearby limestone cave on the terraced hillside that bordered Bethlehem. At that time, several caves on the hillside had been artificially enlarged, creating an upper chamber as a dwelling place and a lower chamber for animals such as sheep. It appears that Joseph found shelter for Mary in a lower chamber, for their cave had a manger or feeding trough intended for animals.[52]

"And so it was, that, while they were there [in the limestone cave], the days were accomplished that she should be delivered. And she brought forth her firstborn son" (Luke 2:6–7). Mary brought forth a son in the

---

[50] *Life and Teachings*, 29; *Israel*, 47; Berrett and Ogden, *Discovering the Bible*, 187; D. Kelly Ogden, *Where Jesus Walked: The Land and Culture of New Testament Times* (Salt Lake City: Deseret Book, 1991), 32.

[51] Ward, *Jesus and His Times*, 18, 20; Smith, *Bible Dictionary*, 157; Pax, *Footsteps of Jesus*, 31–32; Edersheim, *Times of Jesus*, 129.

[52] Ward, *Jesus and His Times*, 18, 20; Smith, *Bible Dictionary*, 157; Pax, *Footsteps of Jesus*, 31–32; Edersheim, *Times of Jesus*, 129.

very "confines of Caesar's attempt at control through counting (i.e., the census)," his empire. Caesar had no way of knowing that the infant born to Mary would be his undoing and the undoing of all the mighty and proud who lord over God's people, for the newborn was the Son of God, the Savior of the World.[53]

In the very act of His birth, God's Son willed Himself to become subject to parents and the traditions of society. Tradition dictated the newborn be washed and rubbed with salt. Jewish mothers believed the skin of their babies would be preserved if salted immediately after birth, before being rubbed with sweet oils. Babies were then placed on a square cloth, and the swaddling or banding process began. Four-inch-wide strips, each five to six yards long, were wrapped tightly around the infant, restraining movement of arms and legs. Jewish mothers believed swaddling was needful, for by so doing the infant's appendages would "grow straight and strong."[54]

The Gospel writer Luke informs his readers that Mary, as had Jewish women for centuries, wrapped her baby in swaddling clothes. But, unlike most Jewish mothers, she had no crib for her baby. Improvising, Mary "laid him in a manger" in the cave (Luke 2:7)

We turn from the manger that cradled the Holy Child to those who would witness that the promised Messiah had been born. For centuries, Jewish tradition held that news of the Christ Child would be revealed from Migdal Eder, a tower near Bethlehem on the road between Jerusalem and the city of David. From this tower, shepherds guarded sheep to be slaughtered as sacrificial offerings at the great altar of the temple.[55] On the holy night of the Savior's birth, like the patriarchs of Israel—Abraham, Isaac, and Jacob—and like generations before them, shepherds were in the fields near Migdal Eder "keeping watch over" their flocks (Luke 2:8). To these shepherds—surely not lowly in the sight of God—the "glory of the Lord," the appearance of the ancient glory, the

---

[53] Gaventa, *Mary, Glimpses of the Mother*, 60.

[54] Ward, *Jesus and His Times*, 22–23; Smith, *Bible Dictionary*, 371; Bruce N. Metzger and Roland E. Murphy, eds., *The New Oxford Annotated Bible: Containing the Old and New Testament* (New York City: Oxford University Press, 1991), 80; Grower, *New Manners*, 62.

[55] Edersheim, *Sketches of Jewish Life*, 76–77; Edersheim, *Jesus the Messiah*, 15.

Shekinah, that was once seen in the Holy of Holies "shone round about them: and they were sore afraid" (Luke 2:9). These shepherds knew much of the Israelite way to care for sheep and the significance of the sacrificial firstborn lambs but knew little of God's glory.

"Fear not: for, behold, I bring you good tidings of great joy, which shall be to all people," announced an angel sent from the presence of God to the shepherds (Luke 2:10). "For unto you is born this day in the city of David a Saviour, which is Christ the Lord" (Luke 2:11). The announced child was not just another baby born to a woman in Judaea or to a wandering people. The Child was the Holy One, the Great I Am, and the "good tidings," God's story. Although the angelic declaration resonates with the ancient Bedouin custom of announcing a birth, "We bring you good news of a great joy, for to you is born this day . . . ," there the similarity stops.[56] As the shepherds listened to the angelic message, "Suddenly there was with the angel a multitude of the heavenly host praising God, and saying, Glory to God in the highest, and on earth peace, good will toward men" (Luke 2:13–14). The announced glad tidings were the gospel message of peace and the Messianic hope—a hope resting upon "the babe wrapped in swaddling clothes, lying in a manger" (Luke 2:15).

"Let us now go even unto Bethlehem, and see this thing which is to come to pass, which the Lord hath made known unto us," the shepherds said one to another (Luke 2:15). Like Mary as she anticipated her visit with Elisabeth, the shepherds went "with haste" (Luke 2:16). How many caves on Bethlehem's hillside did they search trying to find the manger that cradled the Messiah before they found "the babe lying in a manger?" (Luke 2:15). On that night of nights, Mary witnessed the shepherds adore the Newborn King as they saw for themselves what "the Lord hath made known" unto them (Luke 2:15–16).

When the shepherds retreated from the Holy Family, "they made known abroad the saying which was told them concerning this child" (Luke 2:17). Those who listened "wondered at those things which were told them by the shepherds" (Luke 2:18). Could it be that the prophecies of Isaiah of a virgin bearing a son were being fulfilled? Some wondered and others speculated, but not Mary. There was no imagining

---

56 McConkie, *Mortal Messiah*, 1:347; B. H. Roberts, *Outlines of Ecclesiastical History* (Salt Lake City: Deseret News, 1902), 12; Pax, *Footsteps of Jesus*, 34.

or misconstruing of the sacred for her. She knew who the baby was that lay against her breast. She knew of His promised destiny. She knew that the deaf, lame, and blind awaited His cure and that multitudes would look to Him for salvation and the promises of eternity. Yet, she did not boast in her knowledge that night or in the days that followed. Instead, she reverently "kept all these things, and pondered them in her heart" (Luke 2:19).

Chapter Five

THE YOUNG CHILD JESUS

THE RITUAL OF CIRCUMCISION WAS performed eight days after the birth of a Jewish son even when the eighth day fell on the Sabbath. Rabbi Yohanan explained, "It is like a king who entered a province and issued a decree, saying, 'Let no visitors that are here see my face until they have first seen the face of my lady'"—meaning Sabbath.[57] According to later Jewish rabbis, the newborn male was to experience the covenant of Sabbath before the covenant of circumcision.

It is likely that Jesus was circumcised in Bethlehem on the eighth day following His birth, for Genesis 17:10 states, "Every male among you shall be circumcised." The Gospel writer Luke attests to the fact that this covenant was performed upon the Holy Child (Luke 2:21).

Circumcision is one way to show the conformity or obedience of Mary and Joseph to Hebrew law and their belief in the covenant that God made with Abraham (see Exodus 12:48–49). Circumcision is also a sign that descendants of the patriarch Abraham agree to be separate from the world—cut off from worldly enticements that lead away from worship of Jehovah. During the circumcision ritual, the words "blessed be the Lord our God, who hath sanctified us by his precepts and hath given us the law of circumcision" would have been uttered. The father of the newborn would add, "Who hath sanctified us by his precepts and hath commanded us to enter the child into the covenant of Abraham our father."[58]

[57] Dummelow, *Bible Commentary*, 740; Joseph Rhymer, *The Illustrated Life of Jesus Christ* (London: Bloomsbury Publishing Limited, 1991), 30; Pax, *Footsteps of Jesus*, 34, Heschel, *Sabbath*, 110.

[58] Dummelow, *Bible Commentary*, 740; Rhymer, *Life of Jesus*, 30; Pax, *Footsteps of Jesus*, 34; Heschel, *Sabbath*, 110.

After the formal words are spoken and the infant is circumcised, he is given a name. Traditionally, the name of a firstborn son was that of a paternal grandfather. This may explain why some expressed displeasure with Mary's kinswoman Elisabeth when she insisted that the name of her son must be John: "And they said unto her, There is none of thy kindred that is called by this name" (Luke 1:61). But in this instance, following the circumcision of Jesus, a grandfather's name would not suffice. His divinely chosen name, Jesus, meaning savior-deliverer, was pronounced. According to the Jewish ritual, upon receiving his name the child entered into the covenant of Abraham.[59]

Thirty-two days after the Holy Child entered that covenant, "when the days of . . . purification according to the law of Moses were accomplished," Mary and Joseph brought Jesus to Jerusalem to present Him before a priest at the Gate of Nicanor in the Court of the Women on the Temple Mount (see Luke 2:22). The presentation of a son to an appointed priest on that mount, like circumcision, was expected of faithful Jewish parents. The reason for such actions was because the eldest son of an Israelite family had to be formally exempted from duties in the sanctuary. The exemption was done by payment of a ransom or redemption when he was forty days old.

As for Jewish mothers, they were expected to remain in isolation or seclusion for forty days following the son's birth, "which meant that [they were] not allowed to leave the house or to touch any holy objects" because of being viewed as ritually unclean (see Leviticus 12:2–8). These mothers could not "touch anything sacred nor enter the sanctuary till the days of [their] purification [were] fulfilled" (Leviticus 12:41).[60] Then Jewish mothers were expected to journey to the Temple Mount where they could offer a sacrifice for the ceremonial redemption of their firstborn son.

During the redemption ceremony, the mothers were immersed in a ritual bath—*mikvah*—and pronounced ritually clean by a priest. The mothers offered sacrifices as part of the redemption ceremony that exempted their firstborn sons from later Levitical ministerial service.

There were also expectations of Jewish fathers resulting from the birth of their firstborn son. Fathers were to enter the Temple Mount but not

---

[59] Pax, *Footsteps of Jesus*, 37.

[60] "The Story of Mary," *National Geographic*, 20.

if they carried a staff, for a staff would appear that they were on business or on pleasure instead of a sacred journey. They were not allowed to wear shoes on the mount, only sandals. They could have no dust on their feet or scrip in a purse, as such were also unacceptable in temple courts.[61] If fathers met these requirements, they entered the Temple Mount with five shekels, about four-tenths of an ounce of silver, which was required to redeem a firstborn son. Their offerings were carried in their hands, indicating that the shekels were for an immediate, holy purpose.[62]

Now to Joseph, Mary, and the Child Jesus. Joseph would have been one of hundreds of fathers carrying shekels in his hands as he climbed up the Temple Mount. Mary would have been one of hundreds of women bringing "a lamb for a burnt offering and either a young pigeon or a turtledove for a sin offering. If she could not afford both the lamb and the bird, then she was permitted to bring two pigeons or two turtle doves" (see Leviticus 12:8). (Typically, a poor woman offered a pair of turtledoves and a rich woman offered an additional lamb.)

Mary presented herself and her sacrificial offering at the Court of the Women on the Temple Mount. Note that she did not present herself in the temple sanctuary. Women were restricted as to where they could enter or walk on the mount.[63] As to Mary's purification offering, a question arises as to whether Mary literally offered turtledoves or the equivalency of turtledoves as her offering. The question begs for an answer. Inside the treasury building located in the Court of Women were thirteen chests shaped like trumpets—nine trumpets were receptacles for shekels legally due from Jewish males and four trumpets held voluntary contributions. Into trumpet three, mothers of firstborn sons deposited the required money to purchase turtledoves as their purification offering. Throughout the day, a priest took monies from the third trumpet and counted the monies so that the corresponding number of turtledoves were sacrificed. This practice spared temple priests from the additional labor of separate

---

[61] Edersheim, *Jesus the Messiah*, 195; Edersheim, *Temple*, 65; Rousseau and Arav, *Jesus and His World*, 55.

[62] Bruce R. McConkie, *Doctrinal New Testament Commentary: The Gospels*, 2 vols. (Salt Lake City: Bookcraft, 1988), 99; Pax, *Footsteps of Jesus*, 37.

[63] Ward, *Jesus and His Times*, 132.

daily sacrifices and allowed mothers to give an almost anonymous purification offering.[64]

Did the priest, who pronounced prescribed words upon Mary, recognize her as the prophesied virgin and the Child she caressed as the Son of God? Did he think the small infant in her arms was just another Judaean? Perhaps. But not Simeon, a devout and just man, who knew "by the Holy Ghost, that he should not see death, before he had seen the Lord's Christ" (Luke 2:26). He was the one man on the Temple Mount who recognized the infant in Mary's arms as the Redeemer of the World and His mother, as the chosen virgin.

Simeon took the newborn into his arms and addressed God. He praised Jehovah for the unique gift he had received to witness the salvation of mankind. In joyous exclamation, Simeon repeated ancient prophecies that drew upon the four servant songs found in the later chapters of Isaiah (see Isaiah 60–66). These songs depict an unnamed servant bringing justice to the nations, giving sight to the blind, and freeing imprisoned captives. As Simeon begins his own song, he introduces "an element of foreboding not previously seen in the birth narrative."[65] Simeon speaks of the servant being tortured and killed by his enemies. His song concludes, however, happily with the servant being blessed by God and Simeon expressing testimony that "salvation comes by and through our Savior."[66]

In his exuberance at seeing the face of the Son of God, Simeon praises God, saying, "Lord, now lettest thou thy servant depart in peace . . . For mine eyes have seen thy salvation" (Luke 2:29–30). Simeon knew at that moment that Jesus would be "a light to lighten the Gentiles and the glory of thy people Israel" (Luke 2:32). He understood the great importance of the atoning mission of the infant—the "child is set for the fall and rising again of many in Israel" (Luke 2:34). He also knew the future that awaited Mary. Simeon turned to the infant's mother and said, "A sword shall pierce through thy own soul" (Luke 2:35). His choice of the word *sword* has more than one symbolic meaning. Greco-Roman letters of consolation often employed the imagery of a sword when discussing a

---

[64] Edersheim, *Temple*, 48.

[65] Galenta, *Mary, Glimpses of the Mother*, 63.

[66] Dana, *Mary, Mother of Jesus*, 99.

mother's grief over the loss of a child. Perhaps Simeon knew something of the sorrow and agony that awaited Mary as she would watch her Son hang from a cross at Calvary.[67]

But there was no time for explanation of his sayings that day, for as Simeon was speaking Anna, an elderly prophetess, stepped forward. When applied to Anna, the word *prophetess* is a respectful epithet acknowledging an elderly woman who had lived a long, devout, and faithful life. Just like Simeon before her, Anna, who had "served God with fastings and prayers night and day," recognized the infant as the Messiah and "gave thanks likewise unto the Lord" (Luke 2:37–38). Thus, two servants of God—Simeon and Anna—did not need others to identify mother or child nor did they need a priest to remind them of the Lord's promises to His chosen people. These elderly servants recognized immediately the Hope of Israel and knew that the ancient prophesies were being fulfilled. Anna, like the shepherds before her, spoke about Jesus "to all them that looked for redemption in Jerusalem" (Luke 2:38).[68]

As for Mary and Joseph, they did not stay on the Temple Mount long enough to hear all that Anna had to say. They left the mount and headed back to Bethlehem, but not to the limestone cave. They had elected to make their home in Bethlehem rather than return to their village of Nazareth. To many, including Mary and Joseph, it must have appeared that they would be residents of Bethlehem for years to come. But such was not to be.

Wise men from lands east of Judaea—perhaps the Arabian Desert, Chaldaea, or even farther—arrived in Jerusalem searching for a child born to be king. Western Christian tradition numbers the wise men as three. Eastern Christian tradition numbers them as twelve. In both traditions, the men are depicted as kings/magis following the direction of a star in search of the rightful heir of Judah, perhaps in fulfillment of the prophecy: "There shall come a Star out of Jacob, and a Sceptre shall rise out of Israel" (Numbers 24:17).[69]

---

[67] Rhymer, *Life of Jesus*, 31.

[68] Pax, *Footsteps of Jesus*, 40; Daniel H. Ludlow, *A Companion to Your Study of the New Testament: The Four Gospels* (Salt Lake City: Deseret Book, 1982), 269; Edersheim, *Temple*, 23; Edersheim, *Times of Jesus*, 140.

[69] Rhymer, *Life of Jesus*, 26; Ackroyd, Leaney, and Packer, *According to Matthew*, 30; Pax, *Footsteps of Jesus*, 46.

As the wise men entered Jerusalem, they sought an audience with the reigning Roman appointee. "Where is he that is born King of the Jews? for we have seen his star in the east, and are come to worship him," they asked of Herod (Matthew 2:2). Their question implied that Herod, the Roman appointee and exploiter of Judaism, knew of the prophesied star that would appear at the birth of Judah's rightful king. Herod did not know the answer. Their question caught him unawares. He had been so preoccupied with ferreting out threats to the throne within his own domicile that he had ignored signs in the heavens and the ancient prophesies.

Herod was "troubled," and as the Gospel writer Matthew pens, "all Jerusalem with him," at the wise men's question, for it played upon Herod's greatest fear—a "rightful" successor to his throne—an ill omen (Matthew 2:3). There was, of course, the additional element of greed. The wise men were laden with gifts for the newborn king but offered no gifts to Herod. Their costly treasures were not meant for the puppet king, but for a child destined to be King of Kings, whose greatness and power would surpass the inflated reputation garnered by Herod.

For this Roman appointee, whose delicate diplomacy had won the praise of Caeser Augustus and whose might had stopped revolutionaries in Judaea, the wise men's failure to bring gifts to him and their question about a rightful king posed an enormous threat. Herod "gathered all the chief priests and scribes of the people together, [and] demanded of them where Christ should be born" (Matthew 2:4). The learned but unwise men answered correctly: "Bethlehem of Judaea: for thus it is written by the prophet" (Matthew 2:5).

With thinly veiled deception, Herod suggested the wise men "go and search diligently for the young child [in Bethlehem]; and when ye have found him, bring me word again, that I may come and worship him also" (Matthew 2:8). The wise men did not need to search long in the small town, for "the star, which they saw in the east" went before them and led them to the carpenter's home, "and stood over where the young child was" (Matthew 2:9). There in a humble abode the wise men found the prophesied king. Upon seeing the Christ Child, they "fell down, and worshipped him" (Matthew 2:11).

Then and only then did the wise men open their precious gifts that had been carefully packed and carried from the East. The costly gifts, a dramatic contrast from the simple surroundings in the carpenter's home, were not typical newborn presents. They were not toys for a toddler. They were gifts for a ruling monarch—gifts for a king. According to medieval tradition, the gifts were symbols of the royal destiny of Jesus. The wise men gave Him gold to celebrate the King of Kings. (In Christian medieval tradition, gold was the customary gift to acknowledge royalty.) Frankincense, incense used in ritual sacrifice at the Temple Mount and stored in the temple treasury, symbolized Jesus's priestly role as the Great High Priest. The gift of myrrh, a painkiller and an embalming ingredient, foreshadowed His infinite atonement and death.[70] If the tradition has validity, in the gifts of the wise men the divine mission of Jesus the Christ—the Anointed One—was symbolized.

After the gifts were presented to the rightful heir of Judah's throne, the wise men prepared to return to the East by way of Jerusalem to inform Herod that they had found the Child born to be king. When they were "warned of God in a dream" of Herod's plan to destroy the Chosen Child, the wise men did not return to the despot with directions to the child's home (Matthew 2:12). Instead, they journeyed back to their eastern lands and were never mentioned again in holy writ.

When the wise men did not return to Jerusalem, Herod perceived their actions as an affront to his legitimacy as a representative of the Roman Empire. He didn't send soldiers to force the men back to Jerusalem. In a fit of uncontrolled anger, however, Herod did seek revenge. He unleashed his wrath on the small community of Bethlehem—a community that was home to the Holy Family and home to Zacharias, Elisabeth, and their prophesied son, John. Herod knew it was not the wise men who threatened his kingdom. It was a young child living in Bethlehem—a child with a royal destiny. Herod ordered soldiers to slay "all the children that were in Bethlehem, and in all the coasts thereof, from two years old and under" (Matthew 2:16).

The commotion in Bethlehem as soldiers unsheathed their blades to carry out Herod's hellish edict is painful to imagine. Mothers pled for the

---

70 Rhymer, *Life of Jesus*, 27-28; Ogden, *Where Jesus Walked*, 134; Smith, *Bible Dictionary*, 111; Frederick William Danker, ed. *Greek-English Lexicon of the New Testament and Other Early Christian Literature* (Chicago: University of Chicago Press, 2000), 594.

innocent, and fathers, like Zacharias, died rather than disclose the hiding places of their sons. There were heroes and heroines in Bethlehem who protested the heinous crime of Herod, but there was precious little they could do against the soldiers' might.[71] One by one the innocent were slain. Those who could barely walk or question why lost their lives to the unchecked jealousy of Herod, whose every whim was executed with precision in Bethlehem. Sorrowful fathers and grieving mothers saw their offspring cut down by the sword for no reason other than age. The object of the executions—the Child destined to be King—was not found in Bethlehem that brutal day.

---

[71] Ogden, *Where Jesus Walked*, 20; Dummelow, *Bible Dictionary*, 628; McConkie, *Doctrinal Commentary*, 624.

Chapter Six

FROM EGYPT TO NAZARETH

―――――――――

"BEHOLD, THE ANGEL OF THE Lord appeareth to Joseph in a dream, saying, Arise, and take the young child and his mother, and flee into Egypt, and be thou there until I bring thee word: for Herod will seek the young child to destroy him" (Matthew 2:13). Without questioning the angelic command and with the cover of darkness to cloak their escape, Joseph took Mary and the Child Jesus and fled from Bethlehem before the soldiers commenced their brutality on innocent children. The Holy Family did not flee to another town in Judaea where at Herod's whim another scene of barbaric cruelty might be enacted. The Holy Family crossed the wastelands of the Negev and Sinai deserts to Egypt, with the hope of distancing themselves far from the ungodly tyrant Herod. In Egypt, another Roman province, the family found safety in a land dotted with pyramids and recollections of past greatness of a once proud country.[72]

Joseph, Mary, and the Child Jesus were not the first Israelites to flee from Judaea to Egypt. The Egyptian landscape had been riddled with refugee Israelites for centuries. Patriarchs Abraham and Jacob sought refuge there. Joseph and Moses rose in stature and took a significant role in the political structure of that land. The Prophet Jeremiah was forced into Egypt, and Jeroboam fled into Egypt to escape political dangers. The Egyptians were used to hosting Jews, but perhaps never more so than when the Roman Empire ruled with tyranny on a world stage.

Although it had been more than a millennium since Joseph of Egypt and Moses had walked that desert land, when the Holy Family arrived Egypt was still home to multitudes of the children of Israel. In fact, a

―――――

[72] Pax, *Footsteps of Jesus*, 52–53; Ward, *Jesus and His Times*, 31; Ogden, *Where Jesus Walked*, 46.

surprising number of Jewish communities flourished along the banks of the Nile River and the Mediterranean coastline. So many Jewish refugees crowded into the famed Egyptian city of Alexandria that the city was nicknamed "Little Jerusalem."

Although Alexandria had a dominant Jewish population that would make it easy for Joseph, Mary, and the Child Jesus to fit into the culture, Alexandria is not purported to be the residence of the Holy Family. The reason for discounting that city is because it does not fit the river tradition or the employment possibility of Joseph working his trade as a carpenter. Christian tradition suggests that the Holy Family lived in Heliopolis, a city north of Cairo along the Nile.[73] Whether Christian tradition is correct remains to be seen. All that is written in the Gospel accounts is that Joseph, Mary, and the Child Jesus stayed in Egypt, awaiting word from Jehovah that it was safe to return to Bethlehem.

As the Holy Family awaited news, they were unaware that Herod's physical strength had begun to wane. Not long after the tragic brutality administered by his soldiers in Bethlehem, death stalked the despot at every turn. Realizing that his demise was imminent and wanting none of his three errant sons to surpass his greatness, Herod divided his domain between them. His son Archelaus was appointed king over the choice lands of Judaea, Samaria, and Jerusalem. Antipas and Philippus, the other two sons, received less favorable lands. Antipas was appointed tetrarch of Galilee and Perea. Philippus was appointed tetrarch of the territory northeast of the Sea of Galilee. The appointments of Herod's sons, of course, were dependent on the approval of Caesar Augustus. Caesar accepted the appointments and divisions of Palestine, what the Jews called Judaea, with the exception of the small principality of Abilene.[74]

After receiving word of the royal acceptance of a three-way division of Palestine, Jewish historian Josephus wrote of Herod's death in Jericho. While some mourned his demise, Archelaus "saw to it that his father's burial should be most splendid, and he brought out all his ornaments to

---

[73] Ward, *Jesus and His Times*, 304; Rhymer, *Life of Jesus Christ*, 32; Edersheim, *Sketches of Jewish Life*, 79; Berrett and Ogden, *Discovering the Bible*, 223, 268.

[74] Edersheim, *Jesus the Messiah*, 29, 38; Connolly, *History of Jewish People*, 46; F. F. Bruce, *New Testament History* (New York City: Double-Galilee, 1980), 27.

accompany the procession for the deceased."[75] The funeral processional was extravagant, the likes of which had not been seen before in Judaea. The body of Herod was wrapped in precious purple robes and carried on a golden bier studded with rare stones. Paid pipers, professional mourners, a large military cortege, and five hundred servants formed the mournful processional that closely followed the golden bier to the burial site. The garish splendor and pomp of Herod's burial was a marvel and a wonder to observant Jews, who could not restrain themselves from merriment over his death. As Judaeans celebrated the tyrant's demise, their festivities on byways and the outskirts of Judaea nearly overshadowed the expensive funeral cortege.[76]

Missing from the festivities were Joseph, Mary, and the Child Jesus. Surely they had heard rumors of Herod's death, but mere rumors were not enough to cause them to leave the safety of Egypt for their Israelite moorings. They remained on foreign soil long after Herod's demise, awaiting word from Jehovah that it was safe again for mother and Child in Judaea. It was an angel, appearing to Joseph in yet another dream, who provided the needed assurance of Herod's death. The angel directed Joseph to "arise, and take the young child and his mother, [out of Egypt] and go into the land of Israel: for they are dead which sought the young child's life" (Matthew 2:20). And in obedience to the angelic directive and in fulfillment of Hosea's prophetic vision, "Out of Egypt have I called my son," the Holy Family left Egypt and ventured toward Judaea (Hosea 11:1).

Joseph took Mary and the Child Jesus across the Negev and Sinai deserts to the Judaean border. Near that border, when Joseph learned that Herod's domain had been divided among his errant sons, he paused. Knowing that Herod's son Archelaus reigned "in Judaea in the room of his father Herod," Joseph feared to return to Bethlehem (Matthew 2:22). There is little wonder as to why he feared. Archelaus was an unrestrained tyrant with the same evil temperament as his father. Concerned for the safety of the Child Jesus and His mother, Mary, Joseph "turned aside into the parts of Galilee" to a community he knew well—or, as the Gospel

---

[75] Flavius Josephus, *Antiquities of the Jews* (Okitoks Press, 2017), xvii.

[76] Ward, *Jesus and His Times*, 87.

writer Luke penned, "Their own city Nazareth" (Matthew 2:22; Luke 2:39).[77]

No doubt the Holy Family received a cordial welcome as they arrived at the agrarian village where the angel Gabriel had first brought salutations to Mary and where Joseph and Mary had been betrothed and wed. From Gospel accounts, it does not appear that upon their arrival near neighbors or kin had any knowledge of Jesus being the Son of God. Family and old friends of Joseph must surely have greeted Jesus as the carpenter's son. We presume it was safer for the growing Child to be known as Joseph's son rather than the Son with a future Messianic mission. Surely it was safer for the child to mature as Jesus of Nazareth or Jesus, the son of a carpenter, than Jesus of Bethlehem, the target of Herod's heinous crime.

The secret of the parenthood of Jesus was safe with Mary and Joseph. They were not like the shepherds or Anna who couldn't wait to tell others they had seen the Messiah. Perhaps Mary and Joseph knew that not even family or friends could be trusted; it was too dangerous.[78] There had been one government edict issued to murder her son, and they couldn't chance another.

The scriptures give us precious little information about the childhood of Jesus and the role of His mother. What is revealed is that in the rural community of Nazareth, Jesus "grew, and waxed strong in spirit," and was "filled with wisdom" (Luke 2:40). As he "increased in wisdom and stature," Gospel writers assure readers that He also increased "in favour with God and man," for the "grace of God was upon him" (Luke 2:52, 40). Other than these scriptural passages, details of Jesus' childhood are unknown—obscured in silence.

There are assumptions about His childhood, however, that can be made. First and foremost, Jesus was raised by Mary and Joseph in a Jewish household steeped in Jewish tradition. A *mezzuzah* would have been mounted on the doorpost of their home. The *mezzuzah* held a folded piece of parchment on which was written: "Hear, O Israel: The Lord our God is one Lord: And thou shalt love the Lord thy God with all thine heart, and with all thy soul, and with all thy might" (Deuteronomy 6:4–5). This scriptural verse reminded those who entered or left the Jewish home to hear and listen to the word of God. Touching

---

[77] Ward, *Jesus and His Times*, 31.

[78] Talmage, *Jesus the Christ*, 89.

the *mezzuzah* with a finger and touching lips with the same finger was a symbolic remembrance and prayer to Jehovah.

Lullabies based on the book of Psalms and selected prophetic teachings were other forms of Jewish home worship at the time. Typically, mothers sang lullabies to their little ones while fathers taught their growing sons from writings of ancient prophets. And then, of course, there were the elaborate rituals associated with Sabbath day observance. At sunset on Friday, a priest, standing atop the tallest structure in the community, blew on a ram's horn to announce the approach of Sabbath. The first horn blast signaled laborers in the fields near Nazareth to cease their work. Those who worked in town waited until the second blast to close their shops. The third blast announced it was time to kindle Sabbath lights. After candles were lit, three successive blasts heralded the sacred Sabbath day—a day set apart to worship God. On the Sabbath, men and women wore fine clothes, worshiped in the synagogue, and praised Jehovah in other significant ways.[79]

For the Israelites who remembered and observed the Sabbath day, promises were given of God's favor. These promises included Jehovah sending rain in due season, causing the land to yield an increase, helping His chosen people conquer enemies, bringing peace to the distraught, and multiplying a righteous posterity (see Leviticus 26:4, 7–9). Jehovah also promised, "And I will walk among you, and will be your God, and ye shall be my people. . . . [I will] feed thee with the heritage of Jacob thy father" (Leviticus 26:12; Isaiah 58:14).

In addition to Sabbath worship, education of male children was a Jewish custom not to be ignored. After reaching the age of six or seven, young Jewish boys in Nazareth received an education at the local synagogue—the *beit kneset*. Education included learning the basics—reading, writing, and arithmetic. The principal topic of study, however, was the legal observance of Judaism, for "knowledge of God was everything; and to prepare for or impart that knowledge was the sum total, the sole object of education."[80]

It can be assumed that the parchment on the doorpost, lullabies sung by a mother, scriptural teachings of a father, Sabbath day observance, and

---

[79] Franklin L. West, *Jesus: His Life and Teachings* (Salt Lake City: Deseret Book, 1953), 12; McConkie, *Mortal Messiah*, 1:223.

[80] Edersheim, *Sketches of Jewish Life*, 117, 229; Ward, *Jesus and His Times*, 158–159; Dummelow, *Bible Commentary*, xxiv.

education were an important part of the childhood of Jesus. Beyond the typical Jewish customs of the day, however, there is little certainty about details of Jesus's childhood or life lessons of Mary after the Holy Family returned from Egypt to Nazareth. In fact, the next mention of mother and Child is when Jesus at age twelve accompanies Mary and Joseph to Jerusalem to celebrate Passover.

Failing to find answers from Gospel writers, we turn to Isaiah, who writes of Jesus's early years: "He shall grow up before him as a tender plant, and as a root out of a dry ground: he hath no form nor comeliness; and when we shall see him, there is no beauty that we should desire him" (Isaiah 53:2). Although Isaiah's prophetic words are difficult to interpret, it is reasonable to suppose that Isaiah knew that Jesus would have experiences like other boys of comparable age in Galilee and would not be noticed for His striking looks.

With that said, the only other place to turn for details of Jesus's childhood are the apocrypha accounts. In apocryphal writings, there are many fanciful stories of Jesus's boyhood days. The stories always place Him in the crowded marketplace or in the fields and vineyards on the outskirts of Nazareth. For example, in the apocryphal *Infancy Gospel of Thomas*, Mary asks young Jesus "to draw water and bear it into the house." Although Jesus is obedient and goes to the well carrying a clay jug to fill with water, His jug breaks. Wanting to complete the errand, Jesus spreads "out the garment which was upon him" and fills the cloth with water. He returns home to Mary carrying water in His cloth and does not spill one drop. The apocryphal account then tells of Mary keeping "within herself the mysteries which she saw him do."[81] Another tale has Jesus lengthening a board in the carpenter's shop by pulling on it lengthwise. In yet another story, the Boy Jesus claps His hands and dead sparrows return to life.

These miraculous stories point to the goodness of Jesus but lack factual basis. Yet the miraculous stories can be contrasted with vengeful tales that suggest the Boy Jesus had an uncontrollable temper. In one tale, Jesus silences a rabbi for attempting to teach Him the ways of God. In another tale, Jesus turns rude playmates into goats. In yet another, He strikes annoying neighbors dead. As for Mary, in each of these tales

---

[81] "The Story of Mary," *National Geographic*, 24.

she appears in great trepidation and wonder. Are the tales true? These apocryphal accounts and hundreds of others are the results of two thousand years of expanded and embellished storytelling that "mar rather than embellish the childhood and youth of Jesus."[82]

---

[82] Roberts, *Outlines of History*, 35.

UP TO JERUSALEM

THE GOSPEL WRITERS RECORD ONLY one event in the youth of Jesus that puts in perspective His relationship with His mother, Mary, and His Eternal Father. The event was Passover, and Jesus was twelve. The vignette begins as Jesus becomes one of a multitude of devout Jews journeying to Jerusalem "after the custom of the feast" (Luke 2:42). Luke's mention of "the custom of the feast" refers to the Jewish law that required twelve-year-old males to be formally presented to a priest serving on the Temple Mount (Luke 2:42).

The scriptural account tells of Joseph, Mary, and Jesus leaving Nazareth to journey to the Holy City to observe Passover, "a week-long holiday recalling the Jew's liberation from Egyptian slavery."[83] To journey to Jerusalem for the specific purpose of participating in Passover festivities was to pilgrimage if accompanied by others of the same faith—family, kinsfolk, or villagers. Those who made the pilgrimage like Joseph, Mary, and Jesus travelled in a large company often referred to as a *caravan*. Caravans were an elaborate affair made up of neighbors from the same village who elected a leader from among their group to take them up to Zion. When the caravan was ready to move forward, the leader turned his face toward Jerusalem and shouted to fellow villagers, "Arise ye, and let us go up to Zion, to the House of our God."[84]

Joyful followers arose at his bidding and sang hymns of praise from the book of Psalm as they followed their leader up to the holy city. (No

---

[83] "The Story of Mary," *National Geographic*, 33.

[84] Pax, *Footsteps of Jesus*, 62; Rousseau and Arav, *Jesus and His World*, 163; Hayyim Schauss, *The Jewish Festivals: A Guide to Their History and Observance* (New York City: Schocken Books, 1938), 176–178.

matter the geographic location, to journey to the holy city was always to go "up.") Rich villagers drove chariots, the afflicted rode beasts of burden, but most in the caravan journeyed on foot, believing it "more meritorious to make the pilgrimage that way."[85] Whichever way they travelled, pilgrims turned their faces toward Jerusalem, for attendance at Passover was not only a festive celebration but requisite for the people of Judah. Great multitudes of Jews throughout the Roman Empire—nearly a hundred thousand—made the sacred pilgrimage to Jerusalem annually to attend Passover festivities.

Although the pilgrims were a cohesive and joyous group as they journeyed along, once in the holy city pilgrims sought their own errand of worship. For some, the errand included finding shelter in the crowded city. For others, it was purchasing a sacrificial lamb. For still others, it was visiting family and friends. It is not known what individual errands were accomplished by Mary or Joseph. However, it is known that Jesus, like generations of young men before Him, formally presented himself to a priest at the Temple Mount. The priest, upon determining that Jesus was the requisite age, had the responsibility of pronouncing Him a "Son of the Law." This important title gave twelve-year-old men the right to hold a position in a local synagogue, be recognized as a member of their community, choose a vocation, and begin advanced studies. It also gave the young men assurance that their parents could no longer sell them as bond servants. These were the temporal blessings of becoming a Son of the Law. Although these blessings were significant on many fronts, they paled in comparison to the eternal blessing which promised that the young men would dine with the patriarchs of Israel—Abraham, Isaac, and Jacob—at a future Messianic feast. The feast was to be the greatest Passover in history, for the Savior, the Lamb of God, the Hope of Israel would preside.[86]

After Jesus was declared a Son of the Law and other customs associated with Passover were attended to, pilgrims from Nazareth gathered and made plans to return to their village, rejoicing for having been in the holy city. Among the pilgrims returning to Nazareth were Mary and Joseph. Believing Jesus to be among their number, they went

---

[85] Pax, *Footsteps of Jesus*, 62; Rousseau and Arav, *Jesus and His World*, 163; Schauss, *Jewish Festivals*, 176–178.

[86] Talmage, *Jesus the Christ*, 107; Dummelow, *Bible Commentary*, 653.

a day's journey before discovering "the child Jesus tarried behind in Jerusalem" (Luke 2:43).

There are conflicting opinions as to the route Mary and Joseph and the other pilgrims took as they journeyed toward Nazareth. The traditional route places the first stop on the journey as Beeroth, a Hebrew word meaning "wells," which was a day's journey from Jerusalem.[87] Christian tradition purports that Beeroth was the place where Mary and Joseph first discovered Jesus was not among the travelers. Credence is given to this site because of the scriptural saying that Mary and Joseph went "a day's journey" before realizing that Jesus was not with them (Luke 2:44).

It is at this juncture in the vignette that Mary and Joseph leave the other pilgrims and return to Jerusalem to search for Jesus. It is nearly inconceivable that from among the Nazareth villagers not one joined Mary or Joseph to search for the lost youth.[88] The task of finding him must have felt overwhelming, for how would one go about finding a twelve-year-old among a hundred thousand Jews who might still be in Jerusalem? Surely, Mary and Joseph sought the Lord in prayer as they retraced their steps and searched the crowded city for the Son of God.

It was not until the third day of their search that Jesus was found on the Temple Mount "sitting in the midst of the doctors, both hearing them, and asking them questions" (Luke 2:46). Tradition suggests that Jesus was found conversing with the learned doctors in the northeast corner of the Court of the Women. (Ardent Jews believed that beneath the "north-eastern angle of the Court of the Women" was the Ark of the Covenant.[89])

When Mary and Joseph found Jesus talking with the learned doctors, the Gospel writer Luke records, "And all that heard him were astonished at his understanding and answers" (Luke 2:47). This scene of a young Jewish male talking with learned doctors was not atypical on the Temple Mount. Ancient Jewish records reveal instances of precocious young men conversing with and learning from rabbis, scribes, and doctors who had

---

[87] Berrett and Ogden, *Discovering the Bible*, 92; Edersheim, *Times of Jesus*, 172.

[88] Gaventa, *Mary, Glimpses of the Mother*, 67.

[89] Ward, *Jesus and His Times*, 133; Edersheim, *Temple*, 60; National Geographic, *Everyday Life*, 298; D. Kelly Ogden and Andrew C. Skinner, *Verse by Verse: The Four Gospels* (Salt Lake City: Deseret Book, 2006), 740.

written interpretive commentary and narratives of the law—*halakah*, the legal commentary, and *haggadah*, the traditional commentary.[90] What is unusual about finding Jesus conversing with doctors is the Joseph Smith Translation that reports, "[The doctors] were hearing him, and asking him questions" (*JST*, Luke 2:46). This interpretation may explain why "when [Mary and Joseph] saw him, they were amazed" (Luke 2:48).

Yet, Mary had not forgotten her feelings of unrest over not finding Jesus among the pilgrims returning to Nazareth. Mary inquired of her Son, "Why hast thou thus dealt with us? behold, thy father and I have sought thee sorrowing" (Luke 2:48). One scholar notes,

> Although the birth narrative abounds in what might be called emotional responses to various angelic announcements, and although it hints at the pain Mary will feel at Jesus' death, the emotional claim Mary makes here is of a different sort. This is not the stereotypical response of amazement in the presence of divine activity, nor is it a foreboding about the future. It is the real and present terror of parents who do not know where their child is.[91]

Jesus answered His mother, "How is it that ye have sought me? wist ye not that I must be about my Father's business?" (Luke 2:49). His words, the first recorded words of the Son of God in holy writ, reveal that He knew His parentage and true identity. In His brief reply to His mother, Jesus announced that He was not the son of a carpenter or merely Jesus of Nazareth. He was the Only Begotten Son of God and His mother, Mary, the prophesied virgin most beautiful and fair. Yet, Mary and Joseph "understood not the saying which he spake unto them" (Luke 2:50). Surely they had not forgotten the sacred—the annunciation of angel Gabriel, the greeting of Elisabeth, Joseph's inspired dreams, the adoration of shepherds, the joy of Simeon and Anna, or the gifts of wise men for the King of Kings.

Yet, Mary and Joseph knew that it was not time for Jesus's ministry to begin. He was but a youth. Years, as many as eighteen, needed to pass before His baptism by His cousin John and His clarion call, "Follow me" (Luke 9:23). There was still time to nurture Him in Nazareth. Yet

---

[90] Ward, *Jesus and His Times*, 133; Edersheim, *Temple*, 60; National Geographic, *Everyday Life*, 298; Ogden and Skinner, *Verse by Verse*, 740.

[91] Gaventa, *Mary, Glimpses of the Mother*, 68.

what could Mary and Joseph teach the Son of God who had taught the learned doctors at the Temple Mount? As interested as the doctors must have been in this remarkable Son of the Law, they "could not detain Him, for the very law they professed to uphold enjoined strict obedience to parental authority."[92]

In obedience to that law, twelve-year-old Jesus left the Temple Mount and the holy city to journey with Joseph and His mother, Mary, to the village of Nazareth and to be "subject unto them" (Luke 2:51). It remained for Him to complete a season of preparation within a family setting—a setting that may not have been as intellectually stimulating as conversing with learned doctors or participating in Passover festivities, but a setting that was supportive. After all, Jesus was still a youth or as the Prophet Joseph Smith said,

> When still a boy [Jesus] had all the intelligence necessary to enable Him to rule and govern the kingdom of the Jews, and could reason with the wisest and most profound doctors of law and divinity, and make their theories and practice to appear like folly compared with the wisdom he possessed, but he was a boy only.[93]

It is safe to assume that upon the family's return to Nazareth, Joseph taught Jesus the trade of carpentry. This inference is based on Jewish tradition and the *Talmud*, which states, "It is incumbent on the father to circumcise his son, to teach him the Law, and to teach him some occupation."[94] Since Joseph had complied with the first two requisites, the third—teaching "some occupation"—was likely the next step. It was a step that rabbis encouraged by pointedly teaching Judaean fathers, "He who does not teach his son a trade brings him up to be a robber."[95]

If Judaea had been independent of foreign rule, teaching a trade may have lacked some importance in the training of Jewish sons. With the iron clasp of Rome over the heartbeat of the Judaean and Galilean

---

92 Dana, *Mary, Mother of Jesus*, 126.

93 History, 1838–1856, Volume F–1 [1 May 1844–8 August 1844], Joseph Smith Papers.

94 Pax, *Footsteps of Jesus*, 58–59; Ogden, *Where Jesus Walked*, 98; Lamsa, *Gospel Light*, 180–181.

95 Pax, *Footsteps of Jesus*, 58–59; Ogden, *Where Jesus Walked*, 98; Lamsa, *Gospel Light*, 180–181.

regions for nearly eighty years, Jewish sons were not only encouraged to be tradesmen but praised for their acquisition of important skills. Any attempt by Judaean youth to be more than tradesmen—politician, soldier, public tax collector—would disgrace themselves and their extended family. Not many engaged in weeping and lamentation for sons who brought such disgrace upon the family name: obedience to Judaism was valued and disobedience shunned.[96]

Jewish parents much preferred to see their youth in the marketplace wearing a small token depicting a trade than in military garb. The wearing of tradesmen symbols—like brightly colored cloth, large bone needles, and bakers' hats—was expected of new Sons of the Law as much as it was of their fathers. The generational link between father and son in family enterprises was the norm in Nazareth in the days of Roman oppression. It can be assumed that Joseph's carpentry shop had been occupied by his father and his father before him, and so on. Each generation worked their skill and sold their artifacts to the highest bidder at the marketplace.

Christian scholars scoff at artists' depictions of Jesus laboring beside Joseph in a woodworking shop. They do not question that Joseph taught Jesus a trade, but they do question whether Jesus was taught to work with wood. If Jesus did work with wood, "why is there only one reference to wood—a beam in an eye—found in the teachings of the Master?" Adding to the riddle is the fact that wood carpentry was an insignificant trade when Rome ruled over Judaea. Scholars now assume that Joseph taught Jesus the skill of stone masonry.[97] To successfully learn to work with limestone from Judaea or black basalt from the Galilee region was to enter a proud Jewish profession. Stonecutters, masons, and sculptors were highly valued in Judaean society, and learning such a trade would have brought Jesus high praise. It should be noted, however, that despite the number of references to stones and rocks in Jesus's metaphors, we still aren't certain He worked with wood or stone.

We also don't know whether Joseph taught Jesus the trade of carpentry. The Gospel writers make no mention of Joseph during the

---

[96] Edersheim, *Sketches of Jewish Life*, 182; Ward, *Jesus and His Times*, 76–77, 91, 202.

[97] Dummelow, *Bible Commentary*, 727; Geographic, *Everyday Life*, 304; Connolly, *Time of Jesus*, 64–65.

teenage or early adult years of Jesus. Joseph, always depicted in the role of a protector, appeared in New Testament passages up until Jesus returned from the Passover festivities in Jerusalem. After Jesus's return from Passover, Joseph the carpenter is never mentioned again. Although Joseph had protected the Child Jesus from the brutal atrocities of Herod and had been among the pilgrims journeying with Jesus to Jerusalem, his further whereabouts are unknown.[98]

Our only clue that Joseph may have been alive and residing in Nazareth with Jesus and His mother, Mary, is the scriptural phrase, "[Jesus] was subject unto them" (Luke 2:51). The word *them* suggests that both Mary and Joseph were with Jesus following the Passover festivities. Did Joseph train Jesus in the family trade of carpentry? Did Joseph live to witness the Son of God mature to manhood? The questions associated with Joseph's whereabouts are far from being answered.

Christian tradition purports that Joseph died because he was much older than Mary and had had a previous marriage in which he fathered six children.[99] This tradition loses validity by asking simple questions. If Joseph was older and had sons, how could Jesus be the heir apparent to David's throne? What became of the six children when Mary and Joseph went to Bethlehem and later to Egypt? Why didn't the older sons accompany Mary and Joseph to the Passover Feast?[100] These and other queries raise additional issues. Was Mary a widow following the Passover festivities? Was Jesus reared with brothers and sisters born of Mary? These questions and more open the long-protracted Christian debate of perpetual virginity (see Matthew 1:23). This purported doctrine, which maintains that Mary was a virgin all her days, has been debated by Christian scholars and theologians throughout the ages. The logic and reasoning in the debate varies from theologian to theologian and scholar to scholar. What is clear is that the doctrine of perpetual virginity is not found in the writings of Matthew, Mark, Luke, or John nor in the writings of Latter-day Apostles and prophets. What is found is that holy prophets and Gospel writers name sons born of Mary—James, Joses, Simon, and Judas—and write of her female offspring (see Matthew 13:55; Mark 6:3).

---

[98] West, *Jesus*, 18; Rhymer, *Life of Jesus*, 52; Ward, *Jesus and His Times*, 235.

[99] Edersheim, *Times of Jesus*, 252; Ward, *Jesus and His Time*, 235.

[100] Ludlow, *Companion*, 27.

As for Jesus, during the years He was "subject to them," He "increased in wisdom and stature, and in favour with God and man" (Luke 2:52). And as He matured, grace by grace, His thoughts turned heavenward. His profound question to His mother at the Temple Mount, "wist ye not that I must be about my Father's business?" revealed knowledge of His true parentage—a parentage that would prepare Him for His divine destiny (Luke 2:49). The intervening years in Nazareth were preparatory for what lay ahead for Him. The years were a summoning of godly strength required to heal the blind, lame, and leprous and to command the waves of the sea, feed multitudes, and beckon the dead from the grave.

Joseph the carpenter was needed in Jesus's childhood. More was needed than a surrogate father to guide and instruct Jesus as He matured. Little is known of the guidance and instruction Jesus received from on High, but it is known that divine help prepared him to leave His home in Nazareth and His mother, Mary, to enter the wilderness of Judaea in search of His cousin John.

Chapter Eight

MARRIAGE AT CANA

IN A SOCIETY WHERE CLASS distinction, fine-twined linen, and a self-serving embrace of the sacred were all too apparent, a lone voice was heard speaking of something higher, something greater. John the Baptist began preaching in the wilderness of Judaea far from the soft garments and flowing robes of the Jerusalem aristocracy. "Repent" was his clarion cry (Matthew 3:2). Turn from the blatant ills of the Palestinian society was his urgent plea. Embrace the sacred—the covenants between Jehovah and the patriarchs of Israel—was his pressing invitation.

John knew that the time had come for all men to rise above societal expectations. "Prepare ye the way of the Lord," he called (Matthew 3:3). His message was timely and as sure as its divine source. Faithful throngs gathered to listen. Was Mary among them? Many accepted his words and cast aside their evil ways to enter the baptismal waters of Bethabara. She and others did so with the assurance that they were not merely imitating a ritualistic cleansing sanctioned by the Mosaic Law, nor were they following the way of a Gentile to become a proselyte of righteousness. These faithful converts knew that their baptism demonstrated before Jehovah a willingness to make and keep sacred covenants and to begin preparing the way for the ministry of the Son of God.[101]

Yet in their willing conformity, they did not understand the role John the Baptist played in the kingdom of God. "All men mused in their hearts of John" (Luke 3:15). Was he the Christ, the prophesied Messiah, the Wonderful, Counsellor, the Mighty God, or should they look for another? Without

---

[101] McConkie, *Mortal Messiah*, 396; Edersheim, *Times of Jesus*, 189, 355; Edersheim, *Jesus the Messiah*, 41.

equivocation, John stated, "One mightier than I cometh" (Luke 3:16). Although John was greater than all the prophets of antiquity, the "one mightier that cometh" would be greater than them all. For "he shall baptize you with the Holy Ghost and with fire," John prophesied (Luke 3:16).

One day, as John was standing in the Jordan River—a river that flows through the deepest valley in the world as it meanders along its destined route to the Dead Sea—there came a carpenter's son from Nazareth, a kinsman he had not seen since they were both young children in Bethlehem.[102] Although many may have thought the man a commoner from a small village, John did not. He knew that Jesus was no ordinary son of a laborer; he was the Son of God, the promised Messiah.

"I have need to be baptized of thee," said John, recognizing Jesus's divine Sonship (Matthew 3:14). Jesus replied, "Suffer it to be so now: for thus it becometh us to fulfil all righteousness" (Matthew 3:15). John then baptized the Messiah, the Son of Man, the Mighty One of Israel. As He was immersed, Jesus descended in the river beneath all things to enter into the baptismal covenant. And on that day of days "Jesus, when he was baptized, went up straightway out of the water: and, lo, the heavens were opened unto him, and he saw the Spirit of God descending like a dove, and lighting upon him" (Matthew 3:16). He heard a voice from heaven, even the voice of God the Father, saying, "This is my beloved Son, in whom I am well pleased" (Matthew 3:17).

Recognizing His voice and wanting to commune with His Father and "being full of the Holy Ghost," Jesus was "led by the Spirit into the wilderness" of Judaea (Luke 4:1). His purpose in entering the wilderness was to fast and pray and commune with God.

For forty days and nights, Jesus fasted and worshipped God in the desert terrain. As His fast ended, He hungered. Seeking to appeal to Jesus's appetite, the arch-enemy of all righteousness tried to divert Jesus from His appointed mission. "If thou be the Son of God, command that these stones be made bread," Satan demanded (Matthew 4:3). To any but the Savior, Satan's appeal to the carnal might have been enticing, but to one who had communed with His Father for forty days, the appeal lacked luster. "Man shall not live by bread alone, but by every word that proceedeth out of the mouth of God," Jesus replied (Matthew 4:4).

---

[102] Ward, *Jesus and His Times*, 47, 199; Berrett and Ogden, *Discovering the Bible*, 82; Ogden and Skinner, *Verse by Verse*, 88.

A second temptation followed: "If thou be the Son of God, cast thyself down: for it is written, He shall give his angels charge concerning thee: and in their hands they shall bear thee up, lest at any time thou dash thy foot against a stone" (Matthew 4:6). Jesus answered, "Thou shalt not tempt the Lord thy God" (Matthew 4:7).

A third temptation, with the luring promise of riches and power, was hurled at Jesus: "All these things will I give thee, if thou wilt fall down and worship me" (Matthew 4:9). Jesus did not succumb to the satanic promise, for His path was straight and His course toward eternity sure. He was the chosen Savior, the Christ.

Jesus left the wilderness of Judaea to raise His voice along the harp-like shoreline of sweet Galilee. "Repent: for the kingdom of heaven is at hand" was His cry in villages and cities bordering the sea (Matthew 4:17). His message was not new; repentance had been the focus of John's ministry. But His invitation, "Follow me, and I will make you fishers of men," was new and intriguing to those who heard it (Matthew 4:19).

In those precious words, Jesus announced that His preparatory years had passed. The days of being "subject unto them"—meaning Mary and Joseph—were over (see Luke 2:51). Without hesitation, "Straightway [Andrew and Simon] left their nets, and followed him" (Matthew 4:20). James and John "immediately left the ship and their father, and followed him" (Matthew 4:22). Jesus's invitation to Philip of Bethsaida added yet another disciple. Philip, in turn, spoke to Nathanael, declaring, "We have found him, of whom Moses in the law, and the prophets, did write" (John 1:45). Thus, one by one, followers of Jesus were gathered along the shores of Galilee from among tradesmen, the commoners. Fishing boats were put to rest on the shoreline, vocations that had passed from father to son were abandoned, and cares of the world were set aside as men left temporal wants behind to become disciples of Jesus. And as they did, the fame of Jesus spread throughout Galilee.

The first recorded journey of Jesus in which He was accompanied by disciples and others was to the village of Cana. The Gospel writer John records that Jesus and His disciples were "called" to a marriage in Cana of Galilee (John 2:2). Whether His mother, Mary, was called to the marriage feast is unknown. However, it is known that she was among those in attendance.

Whose wedding did Jesus, His mother, and His disciples attend in Cana? Although Christian tradition suggests that they attended the wedding feast of a local farmer, not all gospel scholars agree. A few claim it was the wedding feast of a family member of Jesus. Fewer suggest it was the marriage feast of Jesus Himself. The answer to these speculations is not found in the Gospels. Conjecture over who was married in Cana does not negate the presence of Jesus at the wedding feast or that He "set the seal of His approval upon the matrimonial relationship and upon the propriety of social entertainment."[103]

In small Galilean villages like Cana, Jewish marriages were elaborate and festive—an occasion not to miss. The wedding required the appointment of a chief groomsman known as the friend of the bridegroom. The groomsman represented the groom in making arrangements for the marriage contract and wedding feast. The wedding feast began when the groom, with a myrtle garland atop his head as a symbol of love, left his home to search for his bride. Perhaps Jesus and His disciples arrived in the village in time to go with the groom on his search. With lighted lamps raised high and vials of oil hanging from their arms, they may have scoured the countryside in search of the favored woman. They may have seen the groom remove the wedding veil from his bride's face and lay the veil upon his shoulder. They may even have joined with villagers in exclaiming, "The government shall be upon his shoulder."[104]

As the groom and his bride led a festive procession to their home, perhaps Jesus and His disciples were among those making musical sounds or waving flowers and myrtle branches in joyous expression of the union between the groom and his bride. After hearing the words, "Take her according to the Law of Moses and of Israel," they may have encircled the festive couple as they were crowned with garlands under a wedding canopy.[105]

We do not know whether Jesus and His disciples participated in the traditional elements of the Galilean wedding, but we do know that they

---

[103] Pax, *Footsteps of Jesus*, 89; Berrett and Ogden, *Discovering the Bible*, 112; Talmage, *Jesus the Christ*, 137–138; McConkie, *Doctrinal Commentary*, 135.

[104] Edersheim, *Sketches of Jewish Life*, 140; Ward, *Jesus and His Times*, 115; Harpur, *Miracles of Jesus*, 11; Gower, *New Manners*, 66.

[105] Edersheim, *Sketches of Jewish Life*, 140; Ward, *Jesus and His Times*, 115; Harpur, *Miracles of Jesus*, 11; Gower, *New Manners*, 66.

were in attendance because of the miracle that followed. A large part of the elaborate wedding festivities was the requisite wine served to invited guests. Although water was a precious commodity to desert travelers and parched Judaeans, nothing but the fruit of the vine would satisfy wedding guests. The guests drank freely until the goat carcasses that served as wine bags were empty.[106] Mary, the mother of Jesus, observing that the guests had depleted the wine vessels, said to her Son, "They have no wine" (John 2:3). To be without the fruit of the vine at wedding festivities was more than stopping merriment, it was a Jewish tradition that lack of wine at such festivities brought misfortune on the marriage. It also disrupted the Galilean protocol that demanded guests quench their thirst with wine until the festivities ended.

"Woman, what have I to do with thee?" Jesus asked His mother (John 2:4). Although His words seem impersonal, if not insensitive to the social situation, such was not the case. Anciently, to be called "woman" was a mark of honor and respect, for "to every son his mother was preeminently the woman of women."[107] Jesus addressed the Samaritan woman as, "Woman, believe me, the hour cometh" (John 4:21). To Mary Magdalene, who stood near the empty tomb, Jesus asked, "Woman, why weepest thou?" (John 20:15). In this case, Jesus referred to Mary as "woman" out of honor and respect.

Similarly, He did not excuse Himself from addressing His mother's perceived request in her statement, "They have no wine" (John 2:3). Jesus gently reminded Mary, "Mine hour is not yet come" (John 2:4). The sacrificial hour Jesus spoke of was the sacred hour in which He would offer Himself as an atonement—a ransom for the sins and sorrows of the world. In that hour His unfailing love for all generations of mankind would be tested. Just as the heavy stone of the oil press crushed olives to provide consecrated oil to heal the sick, likewise the heavy burden of the sins and sorrows of the world would press upon Him. That was the appointed hour for which Jesus had come into the world, the hour the angel of the Lord had spoken of years before to Joseph: "Thou shalt call his name JESUS: for he shall save his people from their sins" (Matthew 1:21). That hour for the Great Sacrifice was not to be at the beginning of His ministry. It was reserved for the culmination.

---

[106] McConkie, *Doctrinal Commentary*, 136.
[107] Talmage, *Jesus the Christ*, 138.

The beginning of His ministry of miracles was that day in Cana when Jesus changed water into wine. Jesus, the Begotten Son of the Eternal Father, who had refused to appease His appetite in the Judaean wilderness and had triumphed over Satan's temptations, answered His mother's request by providing wine for wedding guests whose thirst was momentary.

"Fill the waterpots with water," He instructed household servants (John 2:7). Ceremonial purification pots were needed on this occasion, not empty goatskin bags that had once covered a goat's neck and torso.[108] Symbolically, Jesus did not want to case new wine—a reference to the gospel from the True Vine—in the old, stretched skin of Judaism (goatskin bags) that had become brittle with age. The servants, unaware of the divine symbolism or the fact that ceremonial pots would become receptacles for wine, filled the pots up to the brim with water.

"Draw out now, and bear unto the governor of the feast," Jesus instructed the servants (John 2:8). The servants did as He bid. It was not water that was given to the governor, however. "When the ruler of the feast had tasted the water that was made wine, and knew not whence it was: (but the servants which drew the water knew;) the governor of the feast called the bridegroom" (John 2:9). The governor said to the groom, "Every man at the beginning doth set forth good wine; and when men have well drunk, then that which is worse: but thou hast kept the good wine until now" (John 2:10).

This first miracle is unlike most miracles of Jesus because "bystanders do not respond with awe or amazement" to water being turned into wine.[109] Likewise, the governor expresses astonishment at the action of the bridegroom, not the action of Jesus in miraculously providing wine. Although the governor was first to speak of a miracle, he was not the first to recognize Jesus as the miracle worker who changed water to wine. The governor simply thought the good wine had been reserved until the end of the festivities.

It was the disciples of Jesus, the simple fisherman from Galilee, who first acknowledged that in the miracle Jesus "manifested forth his glory;

---

[108] Edersheim, *Jesus the Messiah*, 72; Metzger and Murphy, *Oxford Annotated Bible*, 127; Ogden and Skinner, *Verse by Verse*, 110.

[109] Galenta, *Mary, Glimpses of the Mother*, 81.

and his disciples believed on him" (John 2:11). Their belief was centered in the knowledge that Jesus "brings extravagant gifts to human beings, gifts of abundance almost beyond imagining."[110] As they and the mother of Jesus left the wedding festivities to journey to Capernaum, surely there was much talk about the miracle they had witnessed.

Other miracles followed—thirty-six are recorded by Gospel writers. As the Master and His disciples ventured forth through the byways and into villages near the Sea of Galilee, like the governor at the wedding feast, the recipients of Jesus's miracles were slow to recognize His true identity. Although many were cured of lifelong maladies and afflictions, they could only reply as the blind man, "Whereas I was blind, now I see" (John 9:25). They knew that the stigma of sin that the Jewish culture associated with illness was gone from their lives forever, but few acknowledged it was the Son of God who provided the merciful blessing. While most praised Jehovah for the miracle in their lives and hurried to spread the fame of Jesus throughout the region, some acknowledged Him as a miracle worker but still looked for another to be the Mighty One of Israel to bring peace to the earth. Although they looked beyond the Man for a Messiah to come with power and might to rid the Jews of Roman overlords, it did not prevent them from seeking Jesus at every turn.

---

[110] Galenta, *Mary, Glimpses of the Mother*, 88.

Chapter Nine

WHERE IS MARY?

═══════════════════════

AFTER THE WEDDING FEAST AT Cana, Mary, the mother of Jesus, is mentioned as accompanying her Son and His disciples to Capernaum but not to other villages along the seashore of Galilee. Mary is not mentioned as being present when the blind received sight and the lame walked. Gospel writers do not say whether she was present when Jesus taught on the Mount of Beatitudes or drove the moneychangers from the holy temple. In fact, there are so few references to Mary in the New Testament that following the marriage at Cana, she seems to fade from view as the story of Jesus's ministry takes center stage. Some wrongly conclude that lack of references to Mary signals that she has lost her importance, if not purpose, once Jesus began His ministry along byways and in villages throughout Galilee. Their reason for such a conclusion is that Mary does not utter a single word or take a single action that is recorded by Gospel writers after the marriage feast. They also profess the only time the name of Mary, the mother of Jesus, appears in the Gospels after the feast is limited to "being seen and being moved about."[111]

But let us rethink the issue. Mary is the only person who is present in the prologue to the gospel and in the prologue to the early church. Could it be that Mary's presence in Nazareth, when angel Gabriel announces that she is the chosen virgin to bear the son of God, and her presence at the dawn of Christianity is the link that ties the story of Jesus together?[112] None deny her key role at the beginning of the Gospels, when, as a beautiful and fair young maiden, she humbly replies to Gabriel, "Behold the handmaiden of the Lord" (Luke 1:38). But could

---

[111] Galvanta, *Mary, Glimpses of the Mother*, 43.

[112] Galvanta, *Mary, Glimpses of the Mother*, 72.

it be that by praying and supplicating with the Apostles in the upper room following the ascension of the Resurrected Lord that her presence as Christianity begins to spread throughout the Roman Empire may be more important than we have supposed? Is possible that brief mentions of Mary sprinkled throughout Jesus's ministry may be more than a casual reference to remind readers that Mary is a disciple, too?

The name of Mary is mentioned often by Gospel writers. This has led to confusion, for few of the references to Mary, a common name in Judaea, refer to the mother of Jesus. Gospel writers tell of Mary, the sister of Lazarus and Martha; Mary, the mother of James and Joses and wife of Cleophas; Mary Magdalene, also known as Mary of Magdala; and Mary, the mother of Mark.

Mary, the sister of Lazarus and Martha, played a prominent role in the ministry of Jesus. She was a witness to Jesus raising her brother, Lazarus, from the dead (see John 11:1–45). As Jesus sat in the home of Simon with Lazarus and His host, Mary poured costly spikenard ointment from an alabaster box on Jesus's feet (see John 11:2; 12:3–8). The anointing of His feet showed singular regard, a "reverential homage rarely rendered even to kings" on their coronation day. Among those who observed Mary anointing Jesus's feet was Judas, who was troubled by her seeming failure to count the cost of her actions. Jesus said to him, "Why trouble ye the woman? for she hath wrought a good work upon me" (Matthew 26:10). Judas thought otherwise, left Simon's house, and went directly to the chief priests in Jerusalem—those who could incite the masses against Jesus and lead multitudes to reject their King. The priests encouraged Judas's betrayal and offered to reward him for his sin.

Then there was Mary, the mother of James and Joses and wife of Cleophas. She stood near the cross at Golgotha and was at the tomb of Jesus on the morning of His resurrection (see Matthew 27:56; 28:1). On the third day following the crucifixion of Jesus, she "came unto the sepulchre at the rising of the sun" (Mark 16:2). What was unusual about Mary was her determination to examine the wrappings of the dead and bring "sweet spices" to anoint the body (Mark 16:1). Instead of finding Jesus's body as she had supposed, Mary, like the soldiers who guarded the tomb, saw an "angel of the Lord [who had] descended from heaven, and came and rolled back the stone from the door, and sat upon it. His countenance was like lightning, and his raiment white as snow"

(Matthew 28:2–3). The angel said, "Fear not ye: for I know that ye seek Jesus, which was crucified. He is not here; for he is risen, as he said, Come, see the place where the Lord lay" (Matthew 28:5–6).

Yet another Mary was Mary Magdalene, also known as Mary of Magdala, the very woman from whom Jesus cast out seven devils (see Luke 8:2). Mary Magdalene stood near the cross of Jesus and at His tomb (see Matthew 27:56, 61; Matthew 28:1). "Mary stood without at the sepulchre weeping: and as she wept, she stooped down, and looked into the sepulchre," and saw two angels sitting where the body of Jesus had lain (John 20:11). The angels asked, "Woman, why weepest thou?" (John 20:13). Mary answered, "Because they have taken away my Lord, and I know not where they have laid him" (John 20:13). And after she had "thus said, she turned herself back, and saw Jesus standing, and knew not that it was Jesus" (John 20:14).

The Resurrected Lord asked Mary, "Woman, why weepest thou? whom seekest thou?" (John 20:15). Thinking Him to be a gardener, she replied, "Sir, if thou have borne him hence, tell me where thou hast laid him, and I will take him away" (John 20:15). Jesus replied, "Mary" (John 20:16). Of Mary Magdalene being the first to see the Resurrected Lord, President Gordon B. Hinckley asked, "Why is it that even though Jesus placed a woman in a position of preeminence, so many men who profess His name fail to do so?"[113]

Of the many Gospel references to a woman named Mary, where is mention of the all-important Mary, the mother of Jesus? Most mothers bask in the successes of their sons and want to be present to listen as others praise them. Doesn't it seem reasonable that when curious Judaeans came to see for themselves the miracle worker of Galilee that Mary would be standing near her Son to hear their adorations? When throngs of believers and naysaying Pharisees wanted to know more about Jesus of Nazareth, wouldn't His mother, Mary, have been sought out, perhaps even interviewed?

It is not a stretch to suppose that Mary was in the synagogue at Nazareth when Jesus was invited to speak. After all, it was customary for villagers to be in attendance. Did she witness unrestrained adulation of her Son turn to hatred? The circumstances surrounding this strange twist

---

[113] Gordon B. Hinckley, "The Women in Our Lives," General Conference, October 2004.

in the childhood moorings of Jesus occurred on a Sabbath day, the day when followers of Jehovah in the small village of Nazareth stopped their labors and gathered together in the synagogue to worship and remember the Lord's goodness to the house of Israel. On that particular Sabbath, Jesus joined the villagers and "went into the synagogue," just as He had done on previous Sabbaths in His youth.

Once inside, He sat in the Holy Area, an area designated for those waiting for worship services to begin. Within the Most Holy Area sat the rabbi and other local dignitaries on chief seats. Due to His widespread fame, Jesus was invited to read from the sacred scrolls. When He finished reading, "the eyes of all them that were in the synagogue were fastened on him" as He announced, "This day is this scripture fulfilled in your ears," meaning He was the promised Messiah (Luke 4:21). "Is not this Joseph's son?" the villagers asked one of another (Luke 4:22). We assume that they did not allow Jesus to conclude His remarks with the traditional benediction because of being "filled with wrath" at His messianic declaration (Luke 4:28). They "rose up, and thrust him out of the city, and led him unto the brow of the hill whereon their city was built, that they might cast him down headlong" (Luke 4:29).

The villagers on that holy day of worship, many of whom had known Jesus in His childhood and watched Him mature in favor with God and man, intended to kill him in a Rebel's Beating. The beating did not consist of hitting or clubbing, but crowding him over a cliff at least twice a man's height. By simply crowding the victim to fall from the cliff, no one person could be held accountable for the deadly consequence. If someone were pushed over the cliff by a single individual, accountability for death under the Jewish law was mandatory.[114] Their murderous plans were in place but were not executed, for Jesus "passing through the midst of them went his way" (Luke 4:30).

From that day forward it was said, "Foxes have holes, and birds of the air have nests; but the Son of man hath not where to lay his head" (Luke 9:58). Gospel writers do not acknowledge that Mary was present in the synagogue that day in Nazareth or standing near the cliff attempting to save her Son. We do not know if Mary tried to stop the Rebel Beating

---

[114] Edersheim, *Times of Jesus*, 316; Dummelow, *Bible Commentary*, 746; Ward, *Jesus and His Times*, 235; Ogden and Skinner, *Verse by Verse*, 142.

or pled for her Son's life. Did she assure Jesus that He need no longer wander from village to village because there was a place for Him in her home? Gospel writers appear determined to maintain center focus on the restless existence of Jesus in villages and towns near the Sea of Galilee and on His miracles and teachings instead of retaining focus on Mary, His mother.

If Mary were in Nazareth that day or a future date, there is no record of a greeting or meeting between mother and Son. Yet it is known that Mary was a follower, a disciple of Jesus. The word *disciple* means "to follow" or "to go with."[115] Did Mary follow Jesus from village to village, since Nazareth may no longer have been a comfortable place for her to reside? It appears not. There is only the occasional mention of her in holy writ, such as someone asking, "Is not his mother called Mary?" (Matthew 13:55). There are limited accounts that suggest Jesus had no time to spare for His mother, such as, "There came then his brethren and his mother, and, standing without, sent unto him, calling him. And the multitude sat about him, and they said unto him, Behold, thy mother and thy brethren without seek for thee. And he answered them, saying, Who is my mother, or my brethren?" (Mark 3:31–33). In another account, Mary tries to get close to Jesus but is prevented by a pressing crowd: "Then came to him his mother and his brethren, and could not come at him for the press" (Luke 8:19). Was there not a man in the crowd willing to make room for the mother of Jesus to see her Son?

There are so many questions that go unanswered. Did Mary know of the Apostles' call or of Jesus dining with publicans and sinners? Did she follow Him to the meadows of Bethsaida or to the temple courts in Jerusalem? Was she aware that from city streets to rural byways, disciples and Apostles alike spoke of Jesus as the Christ? Did she presume that nothing could halt or disrupt the healing ministry of Jesus—not element, nor water, nor evil spirits, nor death, nor, certainly, those blessed by His hand? Or did Mary remember the words of Simeon and fear the sword that would pierce her heart? (see Luke 2:35). Gospel writers fail to answer these questions and so many others.

They stay centered on Jesus, the Son of God, and on events that led to His crucifixion. For example, they tell of men who had eaten the loaves and fishes on the plains of Bethsaida being the very men at the synagogue

---

[115] Ward, *Jesus and His Times*, 227; Gower, *New Manners*, 215.

in Capernaum, a village renowned for its grinding mills and excellent bread, who turned their heel against the Master. They pen of villagers of Capernaum refusing Jesus's invitation to eat living bread and never hunger more. "I am the bread of life," Jesus said. "He that cometh to me shall never hunger; and he that believeth on me shall never thirst. All that the Father giveth me shall come to me; and him that cometh to me I will in no wise cast out. For I came down from heaven, not to do mine own will, but the will of him that sent me" (John 6:35, 37–38). In those precious words from the Bread of Life Sermon, Jesus proclaimed Himself the promised Messiah. The villagers asked, "Is not this Jesus, the son of Joseph, whose father and mother we know? How is it then that he saith, I came down from heaven?" (John 6:42).

Such queries inevitably led to the day when Pilate's question was, "What shall I do then with Jesus which is called Christ?" (Matthew 27:22). "Let him be crucified," was the cry heard outside the Antonia Fortress (Matthew 27:22). Crucifixion was the most cruel and hideous of punishments inflicted upon a prisoner throughout the Roman Empire. Crucifixion was reserved for rebels against Rome, delinquent slaves, robbers, and deserters. Surely, such punishment was not meant for a man who professed to be the Messiah. Pilate questioned the crowd's wish for crucifixion. "Why, what evil hath he done?" he asked those standing outside the fortress gates (Matthew 27:23). Without answering Pilate's question, agitated Jewish leaders yelled, "Let him be crucified" (Matthew 27:23).

That day there were but few disciples who remembered the goodness of God to the children of Israel and acknowledged Jesus of Nazareth as King of Kings. Peter, James, and John knew of His royal status, Lazarus and Martha knew, too, and so did Mary, the mother of Jesus—yet they were powerless to stop the tide of evil in Jerusalem. Jesus was condemned to be crucified.

As the Son of God hung from the bar and post that formed a makeshift cross, Jewish leaders—the same ones who had orchestrated the urgent call for crucifixion at the Antonia Fortress—approached Him. They did not come to ask forgiveness for their sins. They had climbed Golgotha to harass Jesus. "If thou be the Son of God, come down from the cross. . . . He saved others; himself he cannot save. If he be the King of Israel, let him now come down from the cross, and we will believe him.

He trusted in God; let him deliver him now, if he will have him: for he said, I am the Son of God" (Matthew 27:40, 42–43).

A condemned thief hanging on a cross next to Jesus thoughtlessly joined in the mockery. Another thief in the same predicament asked, "Dost not thou fear God, seeing thou art in the same condemnation? . . . We receive the due reward of our deeds: but this man hath done nothing amiss" (Luke 23:40–41). Turning to Jesus, the penitent thief pled, "Lord, remember me when thou comest into thy kingdom" (Luke 23:42). Jesus answered him, "Verily I say unto thee, To day shalt thou be with me in paradise" (Luke 23:43).

Such kind words flowed from Jesus's mouth even though derisive accusations from Jewish leaders went unchecked. As Jesus looked down from the cross, He saw soldiers dividing His clothing among themselves, their gratuity for standing guard until the crucifixion process brought death to the condemned. Jesus said, "Father, forgive them; for they know not what they do" (Luke 23:34). As He again looked down from the cross, He saw Mary, His mother. Standing near her were Mary, the wife of Cleophas; Mary Magdalene; and Salome, the wife of Zebedee and mother of James and John (possibly the sister of Mary, the mother of Jesus).[116]

For the first time since the marriage feast in Cana and brief mention of Mary in Capernaum, mother and Son were together again. It had been about thirty-three years since Gabriel's annunciation to Mary and nearly three years since Jesus left Nazareth in search of His cousin John. At this poignant moment, when Jesus saw His mother, Mary, among the women listening to the derisive mocking of Jewish leaders, He exclaimed, "Woman, behold thy son!" (John 19:26). Jesus then directed His mother to turn to John the Beloved, and "from that hour that disciple took her unto his own home" (John 19:27).

When Jesus died, Mary may not have been standing near the cross to witness His death or women smiting "their breasts" or the centurion crying aloud, "This man truly was the Son of God" (Matthew 27:54). Yet she surely saw the sun hide her face in shame, darkness shroud the skies over Jerusalem, and the earth groan in tumultuous convulsions for Jesus, the King of Kings, was no more. Perhaps Mary saw the dead rise from their graves and walk the streets of Jerusalem. She may have heard that the veil of the temple was rent in twain from top to bottom and that fear

---

[116] Dana, *Mary, Mother of Jesus*, 21.

filled the land. Mary must have known that without the Son of God to rule and reign, the holy city reeled in fearful darkness and tumult.

It was three days later that Jesus triumphed over death and the earth rested. As the Resurrected Lord, Jesus appeared to many of His disciples including Mary, the mother of Joses, Joanna, Salome, and other unnamed women. There is no record, however, of the Resurrected Lord appearing to His mother, Mary. Why? After the ascension of Jesus, Mary is mentioned as being with the Apostles in the upper room in prayer and supplication to God (see Acts 1:14). Other than this final scriptural notation, the whereabouts of Mary are obscured in startling silence. To date, there is not a trustworthy or canonized history of Mary. Yet this has not stopped apocryphal writers, theologians, or Christian scholars from filling in her story.

Chapter Ten

MARY REDEFINED

RABBINIC TRADITION CLAIMS IT WAS King Solomon who said, "Of making many books there is no end" (Ecclesiastes 12:12). Anyone who has ever walked through a bookstore, looked through a library, or scrolled through listings of Amazon books can attest to the truthfulness of his words. What is surprising is to find seemingly endless books about Mary, the mother of Jesus. In many respects, this discovery is ironic when the question is asked, *What do Gospel writers tell us about Mary?* A brief glance at New Testament references outside of the Nativity scene suggest the answer is, "We know extremely little."[117] Perhaps a larger question should be, *Starting with brief vignettes in the biblical record—a record that focuses on a patriarchal world where women are depicted as "helpers, assistants, and followers," and too often nameless—how is it possible that books investigating Mary's life, "her theological significance, and her place in Christian devotion" now fill literally libraries and continue to be published at a bewildering pace?*[118] *How could this happen, when neglecting Mary or indifference to her singular role in holy writ is pushed to the background in many Christian churches except at Christmas time, when religious leaders remind their congregations that the reason for the season is more than Santa Claus, festive cards, and hectic shopping?*

The simple answer to these questions and so many others is found in apocryphal writings and the interpretation of these writings that have defined and redefined the image of Mary for centuries. The Mary that has emerged through the passage of time bears little resemblance to the Mary portrayed in the New Testament except she is still the mother of Jesus.

---

[117] Gaventa, *Mary, Glimpses of the Mother*, 3.

[118] Gaventa, *Mary, Glimpses of the Mother*, 2.

For Latter-day Saints, the question is, *Should we give credence to the redefined images of Mary?* Before suggesting the answer, let us review a revelation that pertains to the issue given to the Prophet Joseph Smith on March 9, 1833, in Kirtland, Ohio. While Joseph was engaged in translating the Old Testament, he turned to ancient writings known as the Apocrypha—biblical or related works that are not part of accepted canonized scripture. Unsure as to whether he should translate the ancient writings, Joseph inquired of the Lord. He received a revelation now contained in Doctrine and Covenants 91: "Verily, thus saith the Lord unto you concerning the Apocrypha—There are many things contained therein that are true, and it is mostly translated correctly; There are many things contained therein that are not true, which are interpolations by the hands of men" (D&C 91:1–2). Joseph was told by God that he did not need to translate the Apocrypha. He was also told how to know for himself whether apocryphal writings are true: "Therefore, whoso readeth it, let him understand, for the Spirit manifesteth truth; And whoso is enlightened by the Spirit shall obtain benefit therefrom; And whoso receiveth not by the Spirit, cannot be benefited" (D&C 91:4–6).

Applying the revelation given to the Prophet Joseph Smith as a rule of thumb, we now turn to apocryphal writings that have defined and redefined Mary for centuries. Of the many apocryphal works to choose from, none has had a greater impact on defining the life of Mary than the late second-century text, *Protoevangelium of James*. When the *Protoevangelium* is placed side by side with the canonical works of Gospel writers, the most obvious difference between the two is the focal point of the story:

> In the [Gospels], the stories concern Jesus so overwhelmingly that everyone else slips well into the background. What we learn of Mary . . . we learn by teasing every small detail that the story will yield. In the *Protoevangelium*, however, the background and foreground are reversed.[119]

In the *Protoevangelium*, the sacred purity of Mary is such a profound focal point that little pushes aside her dominance in the text.

---

[119] Gaventa, *Mary, Glimpses of the Mother*, 119.

The earliest *Protoevangelium* manuscript begins with the words *genesis Marias apokalypsis Iakōb*, which translates to "Birth of Mary, Revelation of James." Although this would have been an appropriate title for the work, early scholars gave the manuscript the title of *Protoevangelium* or "Proto-Gospel," because most of the events presented take "place prior to the narrations of the Gospel writers Matthew and Luke."[120] What is tricky about the veracity of this work is that scenes from the Gospels and often the "very wording of the Gospel writers" appear in the text.[121]

As verses of the *Protoevangelium* are presented—1.1 to 22.1—keep in mind the words of the Lord to the Prophet Joseph Smith: "Therefore, whoso readeth it, let him understand, for the Spirit manifesteth truth; And whoso is enlightened by the Spirit shall obtain benefit therefrom; And whoso receiveth not by the Spirit, cannot be benefited" (D&C 91:4–6).

1.1 Joachim was a very rich (man), and he brought all his gifts for the Lord twofold; for he said in himself: What I bring in excess, shall be for the whole people, and what I bring for forgiveness shall be for the Lord, for a propitiation for me.

1.2 [Reuben, the son of the Patriarch Jacob, responds to Joachim by saying,] It is not fitting for you to offer your gifts first, because you have begotten no offspring in Israel.

1.3 Joachim became very sad, and went to the record of the twelve tribes of the people, [and said]: "I will search in the record of the twelve tribes of Israel, whether I am the only one who has not begotten offspring in Israel." And he searched and found of all the righteous that they had raised up offspring in Israel. And he remembered the patriarch Abraham that in his last days God gave him a son, Isaac.

. . .

2.1 Meanwhile Anna [Joachim's] wife uttered a twofold lamentation and gave voice to a twofold bewailing: "I will bewail my widowhood, and bewail my childlessness."

. . .

2.4 "O God of our fathers, bless me and hear my prayer, as thou didst bless the womb of Sarah and gavest her a son, Isaac."

---

[120] Gaventa, *Mary, Glimpses of the Mother*, 106.

[121] Gaventa, *Mary, Glimpses of the Mother*, 107.

. . .

4.1 And behold an angel of the Lord came to her and said: "Anna, Anna, the Lord has heard your prayer. You shall conceive and bear, and your offspring shall be spoken of in the whole world."

. . .

5.2 And her... [months] were fulfilled, as (the angel) had said: in the seventh month Anna brought forth. And she said to the midwife: "What have I brought forth?" And the midwife said: "A female." And Anna said: "My soul is magnified this day." And she laid it down. And when the days were fulfilled, Anna purified herself from her childbed and gave suck to the child, and called her name Mary."

As the *Protoevangelium of James* continues, Mary is portrayed as a child much loved and coddled by her parents Joachim and Anna:

6.1 Day by day the child waxed strong; when she was six months old her mother stood her on the ground to try if she could stand. And she walked seven steps and came to her mother's bosom. And she took her up, saying: "As the Lord my God lives, you shall walk no more upon this ground until I take you into the Temple of the Lord."

6.2 On the child's first birthday Joachim made a great feast, and invited the chief priests and the priests and the scribes and the elders and the whole people of Israel. And Joachim brought the child to the priests, and they blessed her, saying: "O God of our fathers, bless this child and give her a name renowned for ever among all generations." And all the people said: "So be it, Amen."

At age three, Mary is given to a priest in the holy temple to rear. More than one Jewish scholar scoffs at the assertion that a priest raised a young girl in the temple, and they have attempted to assure Christianity that Mary being "permitted to live inside the Jerusalem temple could scarcely be credited by anyone who had the slightest acquaintance with temple traditions."[122] Jewish scholars have made few inroads into the Christian world that accepts the *Protoevangelium* as truth. Yet as we continue the recitation of the *Protoevangelium,* so it was:

---

[122] Gaventa, *Mary, Glimpses of the Mother*, 107.

7.3 [When Mary was three years old, her parents took her to the temple and gave her to a priest.] And he placed her on the third step of the altar, and the Lord God put grace upon the child, and she danced for joy with her feet, and the whole house of Israel loved her.

. . .

8.1 And Mary was in the Temple nurtured like a dove and received food from the hand of an angel.

8.2 When she was twelve years old, there took place a council of the priests, saying: "Behold, Mary has become twelve years old in the Temple of the Lord. What then shall we do with her, that she may not pollute the sanctuary of the Lord?"

The issue before the council of priests is implied—the menstrual cycle or, as James writes, "The onset of Mary's puberty." Should she be allowed to remain in the temple or be given to a man who could protect the virtuous, young woman?

8.2 With the onset of Mary's puberty the priests agree that she can no longer live in the temple, and an angelic messenger instructs that a husband should be found for her among the widowers of Israel.

8.3 Zacharias, Zacharias, [obviously a reference to Zacharias the elderly priest in the course of Abia] go out and assemble the widowers of the people, and to whomever the Lord shall give a (miraculous) sign, his wife she shall be.

We interrupt quoting the *Protoevangelium* to insert words from another apocryphal work, *The Gospel of the Nativity*. According to this work, Mary's "suitors numbered about three thousand." From among the suitors, the widower Joseph was selected to be Mary's protector and "all the people rejoiced with him and said to him, 'Thou art happy in thy old age, since God hath called thee to be betrothed to Mary.' The priests said to him, 'Take her, for God hath chosen thee.'"[123]

Returning to the *Protoevangelium*, Joseph replies—

---

123 Meynell, *Mary, Mother of Jesus*, 35.

9.2 "I (already) have sons and am old, but she is a girl. I fear lest I should become a laughing stock to the children of Israel." And the priest said to Joseph: "Fear the Lord thy God…"

9.3 Joseph takes Mary to his house, assuring her that "the Lord will watch over you."

The *Protoevangelium* then moves to the annunciation of Gabriel that took place as Mary is on her way to a well to draw out water to fill her pitcher. This is followed by her visitation to Elisabeth and Joseph's dream that assures him of Mary's blessed state—

14.2. "Do not fear because of this child. For that which is in her is of the Holy Spirit. She shall bear a son, and you shall call his name Jesus; for he shall save his people from their sins."

The decree from Caesar Augustus, Mary and Joseph's journey to Bethlehem, Joseph finding a cave for Mary, and his seeking "a Hebrew midwife in the region of Bethlehem," follow (18.1). Upon finding the midwife, Joseph says—

19.1 "Mary is betrothed to me; but she conceived of the Holy Spirit after she had been brought up in the Temple of the Lord."

At the birth of Jesus, the midwife is overjoyed and cries—

19.2 "How great is this day for me, that I have seen this new sight."

The wise men then appear, seeking the newborn king and bearing gifts of gold, frankincense and myrrh for the Child Jesus. The wise men fail to return to Jerusalem to tell Herod of the whereabouts of the child born to be King of Kings—

22.1. Herod perceived that he had been tricked by the wise men; he was angry and sent his murderers and commanded them to kill all the children who were two years old and under.

As the *Protoevangelium of James* ends, another apocryphal work *Joseph the Carpenter* continues the well-known narrative of Joseph, Mary, and the Child Jesus fleeing into Egypt to escape the hellish edict of Herod. What makes this apocryphal account so intriguing is that Jesus the Christ is the narrator. Jesus writes, "Joseph arose and took my mother Mary, and carried me in his arms. And Salome followed them upon their way into Egypt; and there, forsaking his own country, he abode a year."[124] The same vignette is also told in the apocryphal account, *The Holy Infancy*. In this work details of the Holy Family's journey to Egypt is presented:

> On the third day of the journey Mary was weary in the desert because of the heat of the sun; and seeing a tree she said to Joseph: "Let us rest awhile in the shadow." Joseph made haste to lift her from the saddle. Being seated, Mary raised her eyes to the branches of the palm, and seeing them covered with fruit she said: "If it were possible I would gladly eat some of these dates." And he said, "I marvel at thy saying, seeing how high grow those dates, and how far out of reach." Then the Child Jesus, being in His Mother's arms, said to the palm-tree, "Bow thy branches, and nourish her with thy fruits." Immediately the palm-tree bent down its topmost branches even to the feet of Mary.[125]

Muslims, who view Maryam (Mary, the mother of Jesus) as a righteous woman, travel great distances to visit the Tree of the Virgin Mary located near Cairo that "bent down its topmost branches even to the feet of Mary."[126]

The apocryphal writings in *The Holy Infancy* also describe an unprecedented, joyous welcome for the Holy Family as they arrive in Egypt—

> The idols of the Egyptians fell to the ground at the passing of the Son of God, the air was full of the music of instruments as at the coming of a King, a new spring of water welled up at the foot of a sycamore tree, monsters vanished, robbers took flight, and

---

124   Meynell, *Mary, Mother of Jesus*, 40.

125   Meynell, *Mary, Mother of Jesus*, 40, 43.

126   "The Story of Mary," *National Geographic*, 58.

the earth brought forth balsam for the healing of the sick. The Child was worshipped by lions, leopards, wolves, and dragons.[127]

There are other apocryphal writings on the early years of Mary and most of the years that followed. In the later years, Mary is depicted as a miracle worker. Through Mary, the "blind people see, paralytics walk, lepers are cured, [and] peoples rise out of slavery."[128] It is not an exaggeration to say, "If scripture does not say anything about Mary's miracles, cures, and appearances," subsequent apocryphal works and the interpolations of these works have created a Mary who performed not only similar miracles to Jesus but the same.[129] There are also accounts of Mary living with John the Beloved in Ephesus in present-day Turkey.[130] Not far from the famous ruins of Ephesus stands the House of the Virgin Mary. Near the house lies a spring "where visitors can make a wish before tasting the water, which some profess has curative powers."[131]

The most famous apocryphal text of Mary's last day is the fourth-century work, *Transitus Virginis*, which is translated to "The Passing of the Virgin." According to this apocryphal account, Mary's passing was a scene of remarkable grandeur, such as the world had never known. The Twelve Apostles gathered from their fields to "the chamber of Mary" in Jerusalem. There John the Beloved assured his fellow Apostles that "the Virgin was near to her joy and her reward," meaning her death was eminent. The *Transitus Virginis* describes her last moments—

Peter stood at her head, and John at her feet, and the other Apostles round about. When it was the third hour of the night, thunder struck the house until it shook, and the chamber was filled with a fragrance so sweet that many were faint and overcome with sleep. In that awful hour Christ Himself entered. With Him were Angels, Patriarchs, Prophets, Virgins, and the Martyrs who had already suffered for His Name's sake. All drew

---

[127] Meynell, *Mary, Mother of Jesus*, 40.

[128] Berryman, *Mary, Mother of God*, 137.

[129] Berryman, *Mary, Mother of God*, 137.

[130] "The Story of Mary," *National Geographic*, 69.

[131] "The Story of Mary," *National Geographic*, 64.

near to the bed of Mary, and Christ said to His dear Mother, "Come, thou chosen amongst all women." And Mary answered, "Lord, my heart is ready." All those present sang a canticle, and Mary herself sang a verse of her own "Magnificat": "All generations shall call me blessed, for He that is mighty hath done to me great things." And Christ spoke, "My beloved, come from Lebanon and receive thy crown." Mary said, "Thou art all my joy."[132]

Mary then passes through the gates of death and the Apostles "set Mary in a tomb." The traditional site of the Tomb of the Virgin Mary is on the Mount of Olives in Jerusalem.[133] In the twelfth century, crusaders built the Church of the Assumption on the mount to honor her. Inside that church is a circular staircase that leads down to a burial space carved out of limestone. According to the *Transitus Virginis*, Mary's tomb is empty because three days after her burial, Jesus visited the tomb and "returned her soul to her body and brought her, alive, into heaven," where she was crowned Queen and Mother of Saints.[134]

Is there any truth in the apocryphal works quoted? Were Mary's parents named Joachim and Anna? Did Mary perform the same healing miracles as Jesus? Was she taken by Jesus into heaven and crowned a queen? For the answer to these and other questions, we again turn to the revelation received by the Prophet Joseph Smith: "Verily, thus saith the Lord unto you concerning the Apocrypha—There are many things contained therein that are true, and it is mostly translated correctly; There are many things contained therein that are not true, which are interpolations by the hands of men" (D&C 91:1–2).

We also turn to the writings of latter-day prophets. A review of their words suggests the story of Mary aligns closely with the words of Gospel writers, not the apocryphal accounts. Latter-day prophets have never redefined the image of Mary as presented in the New Testament except to add insights from the Book of Mormon and Joseph Smith Translation. They have not endorsed any apocryphal writings on the life of Mary or encouraged members to pilgrimage to shrines in Europe that claim to

132 Meynell, *Mary, Mother of Jesus*, 47.
133 "The Story of Mary," *National Geographic*, 69.
134 "The Story of Mary," *National Geographic*, 80, 102

possess relics that once belonged to the mother of Jesus. What prophets and Apostles *have* done is profess that Mary was the handmaid of the Lord and mother of the Son of God. Few have exclaimed their conviction of these truths more eloquently than Elder Bruce R. McConkie, whose testimony I share—

> Can we speak too highly of her whom the Lord has blessed above all women? There was only one Christ, and there is only one Mary. Each was noble and great in pre-existence, and each was foreordained to the ministry he or she performed. We cannot but think that the Father would choose the greatest female spirit to be the mother of His Son, even as he chose the male spirit unto him to be the Savior."[135]

---

[135] McConkie, *Mortal Messiah*, 1:326–327.

About the Author

DR. SUSAN EASTON BLACK JOINED the faculty of Brigham Young University in 1978 and taught Church history and doctrine until she retired to serve multiple missions with her husband, George Durrant. She is also past associate dean of general education and honors and director of Church history in the Religious Studies Center.

The recipient of numerous academic awards, she received the Karl G. Maeser Distinguished Faculty Lecturer Award in 2000, the highest award given a professor on the BYU Provo campus. Susan has authored, edited, and compiled more than 100 books and more than 250 articles.